iPAD SENIORS GUIDE

iPAD SENIORS GUIDE

Master Your iPad in Minutes a Day

A Beginner-Friendly Guide for Seniors

Steve Carren

© Copyright 2024 Sunshine Forest Press

All rights reserved.

Sunshine Forest Press

Disclaimer

The information in **iPad Seniors Guide** is for general informational purposes only. While we strive for accuracy, technology evolves, and updates may occur after publication. Readers should refer to Apple's official sources for the latest information.

Use of any product, application, or software mentioned in this book is at the reader's discretion. We are not responsible for any loss, damage, or inconvenience from using this information. This book does not replace professional advice or technical support—contact Apple Support or authorized providers for assistance.

The opinions expressed are those of the author(s) and do not necessarily reflect Apple's views. All images in this book are sourced from the public domain or are licensed under Creative Commons (e.g., CC0, CC BY), permitting their use for this purpose. No copyright infringement is intended. If you believe an image has been used improperly, please contact us to address the issue. Our contact details are at https://sunshine-forest.org.

By using this book, you acknowledge and agree to this disclaimer. Always follow Apple's guidelines for proper iPad use.

Table of Contents

Getting Started with Your iPad — 1
    What Is an iPad and Why Should You Use One? — 1
    Unboxing Your iPad: A Guided Tour of Its Features — 3
    Setting Up Your iPad for the First Time — 6

Navigating Your iPad with Ease — 10
    Understanding the Home Screen and Dock — 10
    Mastering Touch Gestures: Swipes, Taps, and Pinches — 13
    Using the Control Center and Notification Center — 16

Staying Connected — 21
    Connecting to Wi-Fi and Bluetooth — 21
    Setting Up and Managing Your Apple ID — 25
    Sending and Receiving Emails Like a Pro — 29

Essential Apps and Their Uses — 36
    Exploring Pre-installed Apps: Safari, Mail, and Photos — 36
    Downloading and Organizing New Apps from the App Store — 41
    Managing Storage and Deleting Apps You Don't Need — 46

Keeping in Touch with Loved Ones — 51
    Video Calls Made Simple: Using FaceTime — 51
    Staying Social with Messages and WhatsApp — 55
    Sharing Photos and Files Easily — 58

Boosting Your Productivity — 64
    Setting Up and Using the Calendar App — 64
    Getting Started with the Calendar App — 64
    Writing Notes and Making Lists with the Notes App — 68
    Stop Forgetting with the Use of Reminders — 72
    Voice Assistance with Siri: Your Virtual Helper — 76

Entertainment at Your Fingertips — 81
    Streaming Movies and Shows with Netflix, Hulu, and More — 81
    Listening to Music and Podcasts — 85
    Reading E-books and Magazines on the iPad — 89

Exploring the World of Photos and Videos — **94**
    Taking Stunning Photos with Your iPad Camera — 94
    Editing Photos and Videos Like a Pro — 98
    Creating Albums and Slideshows to Share Memories — 103

Staying Safe and Secure — **108**
    Setting Up Passcodes, Face ID, and Touch ID — 108
    Recognizing and Avoiding Scams — 112
    Backing Up Your Data to iCloud and Staying Protected — 116

Advanced Tips and Tricks — **121**
    Customizing Your iPad with Settings and Widgets — 121
    Multitasking and Using Split Screen for Productivity — 125
    Troubleshooting Common Issues and Finding Help — 128

FAQs — **133**
    Performance Issues — 133
    Connectivity Issues — 134
    App Issues — 134
    Display and Touchscreen Issues — 135
    iCloud and Backup Issues — 136
    Miscellaneous Issues — 137

Conclusion — **138**

Getting Started with Your iPad

What Is an iPad and Why Should You Use One?

The iPad is an Apple tablet computer designed to be powerful yet simple enough for anyone to use. It combines the best features of a smartphone and a laptop in a more portable and user-friendly format. Whether you want to stay in touch with family, browse the internet, play games, or even manage your finances, the iPad offers a world of possibilities at your fingertips.

What Exactly Is an iPad?

The iPad is a sleek device with a vibrant touch-sensitive display powered by iPadOS for a seamless user experience. Forget cumbersome mice and keyboards—interact instead by tapping, swiping, or pinching the screen for an enjoyable experience. Embrace the excitement of technology with your iPad!

iPads come in several models, including the standard iPad, iPad Air, iPad Mini, and iPad Pro. Each model caters to different needs, but they all share the same basic functionality. This guide focuses on helping you get started regardless of which model you own.

Why Is the iPad Great for Seniors?

The iPad is an excellent choice for seniors because it's designed with simplicity in mind. Its large, high-resolution screen makes it easy to see text and images clearly, and the touch-based interface is more intuitive than a traditional computer. Plus, features like voice assistance through Siri, adjustable text sizes, and accessibility options (such as VoiceOver and Zoom) make the iPad particularly senior-friendly.

The iPad also excels at keeping you connected with family and friends. With apps like FaceTime and Messages, you can video chat or send messages effortlessly. The device's lightweight design means you can carry it anywhere, making it ideal for staying in touch on the go.

What Can You Do with an iPad?

Here are just a few ways you can use your iPad:

- **Stay Connected:** Make video calls, send messages, and check emails.
- **Entertainment**: Watch movies, listen to music, or play games.
- **Learn and Explore**: Browse the internet, read e-books, or take online classes.
- **Organize Your Life**: Keep track of appointments, jot down notes, or manage your finances.
- **Capture Memories**: Take photos and videos of special moments.

The possibilities are endless, and as you progress through this guide, you'll learn how to make the most of each feature.

Getting Ready to Explore

Now that you know what an iPad is and why it's a fantastic tool, you're ready to dive deeper into its features. In the next section, we'll take a closer look at your iPad's physical features and what makes it such a versatile device.

Unboxing Your iPad: A Guided Tour of Its Features

Unboxing your iPad is an exciting first step into a world of possibilities. In this sub-chapter, we'll walk you through the process of unpacking your device, identifying its key components, and understanding its physical features. This step-by-step guide ensures you feel confident and ready to start using your iPad right out of the box.

What's Inside the Box?

When you open your iPad box, you'll find:

1. **The iPad itself** – The star of the show, wrapped in protective film.
2. **A USB-C or Lightning cable** – This is used to charge your iPad or connect it to other devices.

3. **A power adapter** – This is for plugging into a wall outlet to charge your device.

4. **Documentation** – Including a quick start guide and warranty information.

Carefully remove each item, keeping the box and materials just in case you need them later. The iPad's minimalist packaging reflects its intuitive design, so you won't find unnecessary items cluttering the box.

A Closer Look at Your iPad

Your iPad is a sleek and thoughtfully designed device. Here's a tour of its main features:

- **The Display**
  The front of your iPad is dominated by its large, high-resolution touch screen. The display is where you'll interact with apps, watch videos, and browse the web. If your iPad has a "Home button" (located at the bottom of the screen), pressing it will return you to the Home screen. Newer iPads may use Face ID for navigation instead.

- **The Top Edge**
  Look along the top of your iPad to find:

    - **The Power Button**: Press this to turn your iPad on or off. A long press may also bring up Siri.

    - **Microphones**: These tiny openings capture audio for video calls or voice recordings.

- **The Side Edges**

    - **Volume Buttons**: On the right side, you'll find buttons to adjust the volume. Press the "+" to increase and the "−" to lower.

    - **SIM Tray (Optional)**: If your iPad supports cellular data, you'll see a small SIM card tray on the side.

- **The Bottom Edge**

    - **Charging Port**: This is where you connect your charging cable. Depending on your model, this may be a USB-C or Lightning port.

    - **Speakers**: Located near the charging port, these deliver rich audio for music and videos.

- **The Back Panel**
  Flip your iPad over to find:

    - **The Rear Camera**: Perfect for capturing photos and videos.

    - **Apple Logo**: A simple yet iconic mark that reflects the quality of the device.

Turning Your iPad On for the First Time

1. **Locate the Power Button**: On the top edge of your iPad, press and hold the Power button until you see the Apple logo appear on the screen.

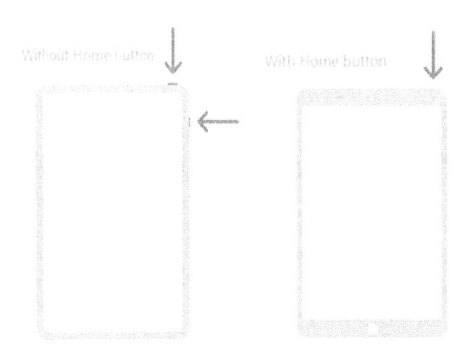

2. **Wait for the Setup Screen**: Once the logo disappears, you'll be greeted with a welcome screen displaying "Hello" in multiple languages. This indicates your iPad is ready to be set up.

Tips for a Successful Unboxing Experience

- **Prepare a Workspace**: Unbox your iPad on a clean, flat surface to avoid dropping or damaging it.

- **Inspect for Damage**: Check your device and accessories for any visible defects. If something seems off, contact Apple support immediately.

- **Charge Before Use**: Although iPads often come partially charged, it's a good idea to fully charge your device before beginning the setup process.

Setting Up Your iPad for the First Time

Setting up your iPad for the first time is a straightforward process designed to help you personalize your device and connect it to the tools and features you'll use daily. This sub-chapter will guide you step-by-step through the setup process, ensuring that your iPad is ready to meet your specific needs.

Step 1: Powering On Your iPad

To begin:

1. Press and hold the **Power button** (located on the top edge of your iPad) until the Apple logo appears.

2. Wait a moment for the **Welcome screen**, which displays "Hello" in multiple languages.

Once you see the welcome screen, swipe upward (You can also tap the Home button on older models for quick access!) to start.

Step 2: Choosing Your Language and Region

You'll first be prompted to select your preferred language. Scroll through the list and tap on the language you're most comfortable with. Next, select your region or country. This ensures your iPad is set up for local time, currency, and other regional settings.

Step 3: Connecting to Wi-Fi

To access most of your iPad's features, you'll need an internet connection:

1. Select your Wi-Fi network from the list on the screen.

2. To connect to the network, enter the password using the on-screen keyboard and then tap "Join."

3. No Wi-Fi? No worries! You can skip this step and connect later, but keep in mind that some setup features might need an internet connection.

Step 4: Setting Up Face ID, Touch ID, or Passcode

Your iPad offers several security options to protect your data:

- **Face ID**: If your iPad supports Face ID, you'll be prompted to scan your face by moving your head in a circular motion while following on-screen instructions.

- **Touch ID**: For devices with a Home button, you can set up Touch ID by placing your finger on the button repeatedly until the device captures your fingerprint.

- **Passcode**: Even if you set up Face ID or Touch ID, you'll also need to create a passcode as a backup. Choose a code you can remember but that is difficult for others to guess.

Step 5: Signing In with Your Apple ID

An Apple ID is essential for accessing features like the App Store, iCloud, and FaceTime. If you already have an Apple ID:

1. Enter your Apple ID email and password.

2. Get ready to verify your identity! Simply follow the prompts and keep an eye out for a code sent straight to your email or phone.

If you don't have an Apple ID:

1. Tap Create a Free Apple ID and follow the instructions to set one up.

2. You'll need to provide your name, birth date, and an email address.

Step 6: Enabling iCloud and Other Features

During setup, you'll be asked whether you'd like to enable **iCloud**, Apple's cloud storage service. Enabling iCloud allows you to:

- Take control of your data—automatically back up your photos, documents, and settings.

- Sync your data across all your Apple devices. You'll also have options to enable features like Find My iPad (to locate your device if it's lost) and **iCloud Drive** (for file storage).

Step 7: Customizing Your Settings

You'll now have the opportunity to configure additional features, such as:

- **Siri**: Apple's voice assistant, which can help you perform tasks using voice commands.

- **Screen Time**: A tool for monitoring your usage habits and setting limits if desired.

- **Automatic Updates**: Allow your iPad to install updates automatically to keep your device secure and up-to-date.

Step 8: Completing Setup

Once you've finished selecting your preferences, your iPad will display a confirmation screen. Tap **Get Started** to proceed to the Home screen. You're now ready to explore your new device!

Tips for a Smooth Setup

- **Have Your Information Ready**: Before starting, ensure you have your Wi-Fi password and Apple ID details on hand.
- **Take Your Time**: The setup process is designed to guide you step by step, so there's no need to rush.
- **Ask for Help**: If you get stuck, don't hesitate to ask a family member or friend or visit Apple's support website.

Congratulations! Your iPad is now ready for use. In the next chapter, we'll dive deeper into the iPad's navigation and features to help you feel at home with your new device.

Navigating Your iPad with Ease

Understanding the Home Screen and Dock

The Home Screen is the central hub of your iPad. It's where you'll access your apps, widgets, and key tools, and it serves as the starting point for everything you do. Alongside the Home Screen, the Dock—a versatile toolbar located at the bottom—allows quick access to frequently used apps and multitasking features. In this sub-chapter, we'll break down the Home Screen and Dock so you feel confident navigating them.

What Is the Home Screen?

The Home Screen is the first thing you see after unlocking your iPad. It's designed to keep your apps and widgets organized for easy access. Think of it as the digital equivalent of your desk: everything you need is laid out in plain view, and you can arrange it however you like.

Key Features of the Home Screen:

1. **App Icons**: These are the small, square images that represent your apps. Tapping an app icon opens it.

2. **Widgets**: Widgets are dynamic, interactive tiles that display live information, such as the weather, your calendar, or news headlines.

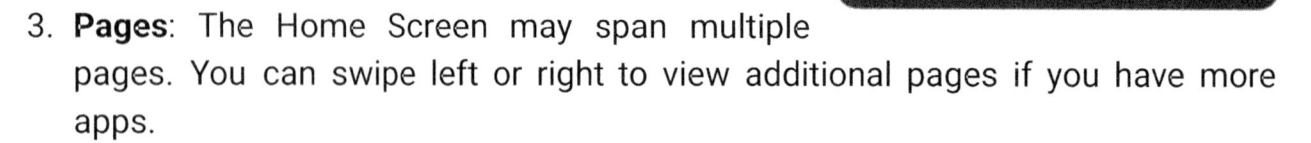

3. **Pages**: The Home Screen may span multiple pages. You can swipe left or right to view additional pages if you have more apps.

Navigating the Home Screen

1. **Unlocking Your iPad**: Once you unlock your device using Face ID, Touch ID, or a passcode, the Home Screen appears.

2. **Opening an App**: Tap once on an app icon to open it.

3. **Returning to the Home Screen**:
    - On devices with a Home button, press it once to return.
    - On devices without a Home button, swipe up from the bottom edge of the screen.

Organizing the Home Screen

The iPad allows you to customize the layout of your Home Screen:

- **Moving Apps**:
    1. Press and hold any app icon until the icons begin to jiggle.
    2. Drag the app to a new location or another page.
    3. Tap Done (in the top-right corner) to save the changes.
- **Creating Folders**: To create a folder, drag one app on top of another. This is an effective method to group similar apps, like social media or productivity tools.
- **Adding Widgets**: Swipe right on the Home Screen to access the widget area. Tap **Edit** or the **+** icon to add or customize widgets.

What Is the Dock?

The Dock is the toolbar at the bottom of the screen that stays visible no matter which page of the Home Screen you're on. It offers easy access to your favorite apps and those you have recently used, making multitasking effortless.

Key Features of the Dock:

1. **Pinned Apps**: On the left side of the Dock, you can pin apps you use frequently.

2. **Recently Used Apps**: The right side of the Dock displays apps you've recently opened or apps suggested by Siri.

3. **Multitasking Tools**: The Dock is essential for opening multiple apps at once or using Split View (covered in later chapters).

Using the Dock

1. **Accessing the Dock**:
   - From the Home Screen, the Dock is always visible.
   - Within an app, swipe up gently from the bottom edge of the screen to reveal the Dock.

2. **Opening an App from the Dock**: Tap any app icon on the Dock to open it immediately.

3. **Customizing the Dock**:
   - Drag apps to or from the Dock to add or remove them.
   - The Dock on most iPads can hold up to 13 apps.

Tips for Mastering the Home Screen and Dock

- **Experiment with Widgets**: Widgets can save time by showing you useful information at a glance, such as your next calendar appointment or the latest news.

- **Keep It Simple**: Start with a clean Home Screen by pinning only the apps you use most often. You can always add more later.

- **Use the Dock for Efficiency**: Place your most-used apps (like Mail, Safari, or Messages) in the Dock to minimize searching.

The Home Screen and Dock are designed to make your iPad experience intuitive and efficient. With these basics in place, you're ready to explore more advanced navigation features in the next sub-chapter.

Mastering Touch Gestures: Swipes, Taps, and Pinches

The iPad's touch screen is your gateway to interacting with apps, navigating menus, and performing tasks. Unlike traditional devices with keyboards or a mouse, the iPad relies on intuitive gestures like swiping, tapping, and pinching. Mastering these gestures will help you use your device effortlessly and confidently. This sub-chapter breaks down the essential touch gestures and explains when and how to use them.

The Basics of Touch Gestures

At its core, the iPad responds to the way you touch and move your fingers on the screen. Every gesture is designed to mimic natural motions, making it easy to learn—even if you're new to touch screens. Let's start with the three foundational gestures: **swipes, taps, and pinches**.

Swipes: Moving Through the iPad

Swiping is the action of sliding your finger across the screen. It's one of the most versatile gestures, used for navigating menus, scrolling through content, and more.

Key Swipes to Practice:

1. **Swipe Left or Right**:
    - **Purpose**: Move between Home Screen pages or switch photos in your gallery.
    - **How to Do It**: Place your finger on the screen and move it horizontally in one smooth motion.

Swipe Right   Swipe Left

2. **Swipe Up**:

    - **Purpose**: Return to the Home Screen or reveal the Dock when inside an app.

    - **How to Do It**: Starting at the bottom edge of the screen, slide your finger upward.

    - **Advanced Tip**: A small swipe reveals the Dock, while a full swipe takes you back to the Home Screen.

3. **Swipe Down**:

    - **Purpose**: Open Notification Center or Search.

    - **How to Do It**:

        - Swipe down from the very top of the screen to view notifications.

        - Swipe down from the center of the Home Screen to access the search bar.

Taps: The Digital "Click"

Tapping is the equivalent of clicking a button on a computer mouse. It's how you select apps, press buttons, and interact with most features.

Types of Taps:

1. **Single Tap**:

    - **Purpose**: Open an app, select an option, or confirm an action.

    - **How to Do It**: Lightly touch the screen with the tip of your finger.

2. **Double Tap**:
   - **Purpose**: Zoom in on photos or web pages (in certain apps).
   - **How to Do It**: Tap the same spot twice in quick succession.

3. **Tap and Hold (Long Press)**:
   - **Purpose**: Access additional options, such as rearranging apps or opening context menus.
   - **How to Do It**: Press and hold your finger on an icon or element until options appear.

Pinches: Zooming In and Out

Pinching is used to change the size of images, text, or web pages, allowing you to zoom in for a closer look or zoom out to see more.

How to Pinch:

1. **Zoom In**:
   - **Purpose**: Magnify text, images, or maps.
   - **How to Do It**: Place two fingers (thumb and index finger work best) on the screen close together, then spread them apart.

2. **Zoom Out**:
   - **Purpose**: Shrink the view to see more of the screen or fit content into one view.
   - **How to Do It**: Place two fingers on the screen farther apart, then pinch them together.

Combining Gestures for Efficiency

Once you're comfortable with basic gestures, you can combine them to perform tasks more efficiently:

- **Swipe Up and Hold**: Access the App Switcher to view and switch between recently used apps.

- **Pinch with Five Fingers**: Return to the Home Screen without using the Dock or Home button.

- **Swipe Left or Right with Four Fingers**: Quickly switch between open apps.

Tips for Mastering Touch Gestures

- **Practice Makes Perfect**: Spend time exploring your iPad by opening apps, zooming in on photos, and swiping between pages.

- **Use a Light Touch**: The iPad's screen is highly responsive; there's no need to press hard.

- **Experiment Safely**: You can't "break" anything by experimenting with gestures, so feel free to explore.

- **Clean the Screen**: A clean screen ensures better accuracy when performing gestures. Make sure to wipe it regularly with a soft, lint-free cloth.

By mastering swipes, taps, and pinches, you've taken an important step toward unlocking the full potential of your iPad. These simple yet powerful gestures will serve as the foundation for navigating apps, browsing the web, and interacting with your device.

Using the Control Center and Notification Center

The Control Center and Notification Center are two essential features of your iPad that give you quick access to important tools and information. The Control Center provides shortcuts for settings and frequently used features, while the Notification Center organizes alerts, reminders, and updates from your apps. Mastering these tools will help you stay informed and in control of your device.

What Is the Control Center?

The Control Center is a menu of shortcuts. This includes frequently used functions, such as adjusting brightness, turning Wi-Fi on or off, and controlling music playback. Instead of navigating through multiple settings, the Control Center allows you to access these features instantly.

Accessing the Control Center

To open the Control Center:

1. **On iPads Without a Home Button**: Swipe down from the upper-right corner of the screen.

2. **On iPads with a Home Button**: Swipe up from the bottom edge of the screen.

To close the Control Center, swipe up from the bottom or tap anywhere outside the menu.

Features of the Control Center

The Control Center is fully customizable, but here are the default features you'll find:

1. **Brightness Slider**: Adjust your screen's brightness.

2. **Volume Slider**: Controls the volume of your device.

3. **Wi-Fi and Bluetooth Toggles**: Quickly enable or disable wireless connections.

4. **Airplane Mode:** Turn off all wireless connections with a single tap.

5. **Do Not Disturb**: Silence notifications temporarily.

6. **Music Controls:** Play, pause, or skip tracks.

7. **Flashlight, Timer, and Camera Shortcuts**: Access these tools instantly.

Customizing the Control Center

You can tailor the Control Center to include the shortcuts you use most often:

1. Open the **Settings** app.

2. Tap **Control Center**.

3. Select **Customize Controls**.

4. Add or remove shortcuts by tapping the + or - icons next to each option.

For example, you might add shortcuts for **Screen Recording**, **Low Power Mode**, or a **calculator**.

What Is the Notification Center?

The Notification Center is where you'll find all your alerts, including messages, reminders, app updates, and calendar notifications. It organizes this information so you can review it at your convenience.

Accessing the Notification Center

1. **To View Notifications**: Swipe down from the very top of the screen.

2. **To Close the Notification Center**: Swipe up from the bottom of the screen or tap anywhere outside the list of notifications.

If your iPad is locked, you can still access the Notification Center by swiping down from the top of the Lock Screen.

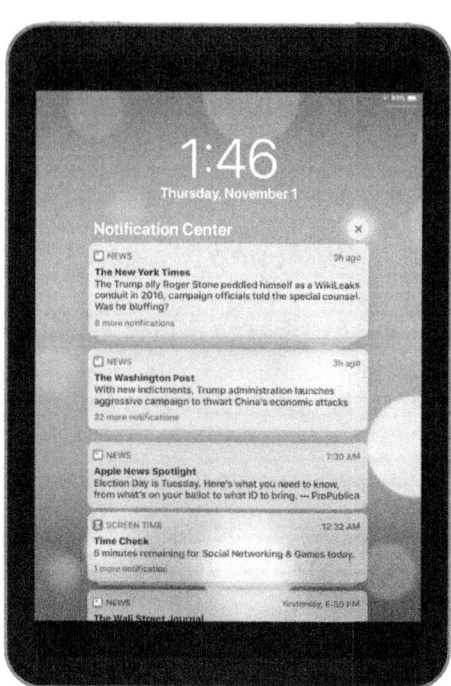

Managing Notifications

Notifications can be dismissed, acted upon, or cleared entirely:

1. **Interacting with a Notification**: Tap a notification to open the associated app. For instance, tapping a message alert will open the Messages app.

2. **Dismissing a Notification**: Swipe a notification to the left and tap Clear.

3. **Clearing All Notifications**: Tap and hold the X at the top of the Notification Center, then select Clear All Notifications.

Customizing Notification Preferences

Take charge of your notifications! You have the power to customize which apps can send them and decide how they show up on your device:

1. Open the **Settings** app.

2. Tap **Notifications**.

3. Select an app from the list to adjust its notification settings, such as enabling or disabling sounds, badges, and banners.

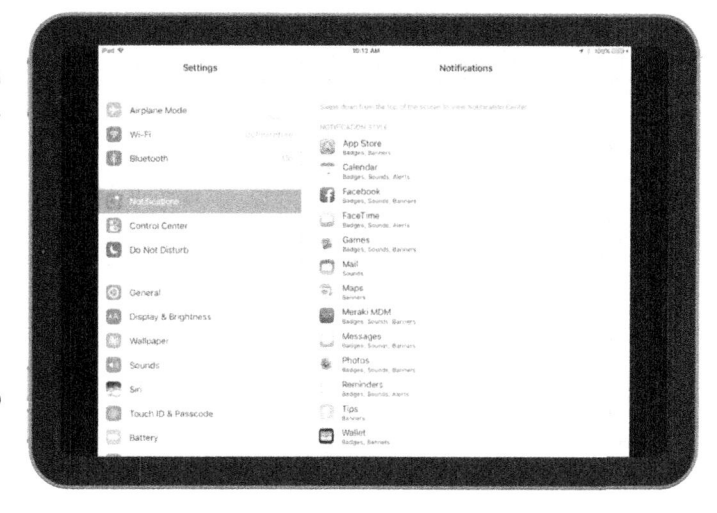

Using Both Centers Together

The Control Center and Notification Center are designed to complement each other:

- Use the **Control Center** to take immediate action, such as enabling Do Not Disturb to silence incoming alerts.

- Review past alerts or missed calls in the **Notification Center** without feeling rushed.

Tips for Mastering the Control Center and Notification Center

- **Practice Accessing Them**: Spend a few minutes swiping to open and close both menus. Muscle memory will make this second nature.

- **Keep Notifications Organized**: Review and clear notifications regularly to prevent clutter.

- **Customize to Your Needs**: Adjust the Control Center and Notification preferences to suit your daily routine.

By understanding how to use the Control Center and Notification Center, you'll unlock a new level of convenience and efficiency on your iPad. These tools keep your most important features and information just a swipe away.

Staying Connected

Connecting to Wi-Fi and Bluetooth

Staying connected is essential to getting the most out of your iPad. Whether you're browsing the internet, sharing photos with family, or using wireless headphones, your iPad relies on Wi-Fi and Bluetooth to keep you linked to the digital world. This sub-chapter will guide you step-by-step through connecting to Wi-Fi networks and pairing Bluetooth devices.

What Is Wi-Fi, and Why Is It Important?

With Wi-Fi, your iPad can effortlessly connect to the internet wirelessly. From reading emails to streaming videos, most iPad activities require an internet connection. Setting up Wi-Fi is one of the first steps to ensure your device works effectively.

How to Connect to Wi-Fi

1. **Open Settings**:
   - Tap the Settings app, which looks like a gray gear.

2. **Select Wi-Fi**:
   - In the left-hand menu, tap Wi-Fi.

3. **Turn On Wi-Fi**:
   - If the Wi-Fi toggle is off, tap it to switch it on. It should turn green.

4. **Choose a Network**:
   - Your iPad will show a list of available Wi-Fi networks.
   - Tap the name of the network you want to join.

5. **Enter the Password**:

- iPad Seniors Guide -

- If the network is secured, you will need to enter a password to gain access.
- Type the password using the keyboard and tap Join.

6. **Confirm Connection**:

- Once you are connected, a checkmark will appear next to the name of the network, and a Wi-Fi symbol will appear in the upper-right corner of the screen.

Troubleshooting Tip: If the network doesn't appear, ensure you're within range, or try restarting your router.

What Is Bluetooth and Why Use It?

Bluetooth is an innovative wireless technology that lets your iPad connect to other devices, such as keyboards, headphones, or speakers. It's ideal for creating a clutter-free environment and enhancing your iPad's functionality.

How to Turn On Bluetooth

1. **Open Settings**:

    - Tap the Settings app.

2. **Select Bluetooth**:

    - In the left-hand menu, tap Bluetooth.

3. **Turn On Bluetooth**:

    - Toggle the switch to turn on Bluetooth. It should turn green, and your iPad will start searching for nearby Bluetooth devices.

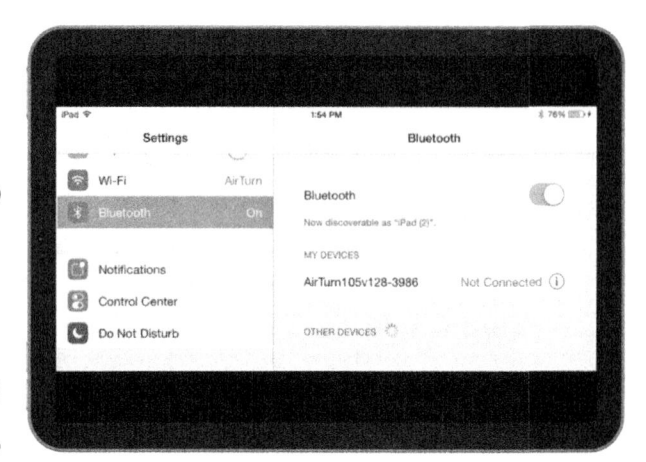

How to Pair a Bluetooth Device

1. **Prepare the Device:**

   - Ensure the device you want to connect (e.g., headphones or a keyboard) is turned on and in pairing mode. Refer to the device's manual for instructions on enabling pairing mode.

2. **Select the Device:**

   - Under the list of available devices, tap the name of the device you want to pair with.

3. **Confirm the Pairing Request:**

   - You may need to enter a code or confirm the pairing request on both devices to establish a secure connection. Follow the on-screen instructions.

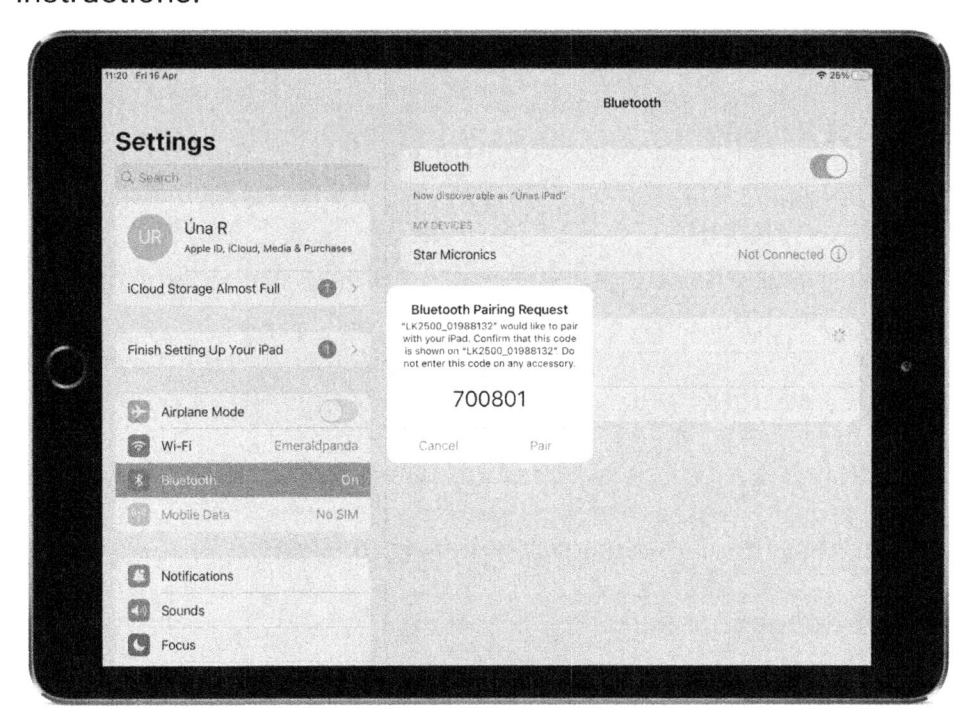

4. **Verify Connection:**

   - Once paired, the device will appear under My Devices with the status Connected.

Pro Tip: For better battery life, turn off Bluetooth when you're not using it.

Managing Your Connections

1. **Switching Networks**:

    - If you move between locations with different Wi-Fi networks, go to Settings > Wi-Fi and select the desired network.

2. **Removing Bluetooth Devices**:

    - To disconnect a paired device, tap the i icon next to its name in Settings > Bluetooth and select Forget This Device.

3. **Airplane Mode**:

    - When traveling, you can temporarily disable Wi-Fi and Bluetooth by enabling Airplane Mode in the Control Center or Settings.

Common Problems and Solutions

1. **Wi-Fi Isn't Connecting**:

    - Ensure you've entered the correct password.

    - Restart your iPad by pressing and holding the Power button until you see the power-off slider.

2. **Bluetooth Device not Found**:

    - Make sure the device is in pairing mode and close to your iPad.

    - Check that Bluetooth is enabled on your iPad.

3. **Intermittent Connections**:

    - Move closer to your Wi-Fi router or Bluetooth device to avoid signal interference.

Tips for Staying Secure While Connected

- **Connect to Secure Wi-Fi Networks:** Avoid using public Wi-Fi networks that don't require a password, as they may not be secure.

- **Turn Off Sharing**: When using public Wi-Fi, disable file sharing to protect your personal data.

- **Keep Software Updated**: Regular updates often include security improvements. Go to **Settings > General > Software Update** to check for updates.

By understanding how to connect to Wi-Fi and Bluetooth, you've unlocked two of the most powerful tools on your iPad. Whether you're enjoying your favorite music on wireless headphones or surfing the web, staying connected is key to enjoying your device to the fullest.

Setting Up and Managing Your Apple ID

Your Apple ID is the key to unlocking the full potential of your iPad. It serves as your personal account for accessing Apple services such as the App Store, iCloud, FaceTime, and more. In this sub-chapter, we'll walk you through setting up your Apple ID, managing it effectively, and ensuring it remains secure.

What Is an Apple ID?

An Apple ID is your unique account that connects you to Apple's ecosystem. It allows you to:

- Unlock a world of entertainment by downloading apps, music, and movies from the App Store and iTunes.

- Sync data like contacts, photos, and notes across your devices using iCloud.

- Use services such as FaceTime and iMessage for seamless communication.

- Securely back up your device.

Without an Apple ID, many of the iPad's most useful features won't be accessible.

Setting Up Your Apple ID

If you don't already have an Apple ID, you'll need to create one. Here's how:

1. **Open Settings**:
   - Tap the Settings app, which looks like a gray gear.

2. **Tap 'Sign In to Your iPad'**:
   - You'll find this option at the top of the Settings menu.

3. **Select 'Don't Have an Apple ID or Forgot It?'**
   - Tap this option and choose Create Apple ID.

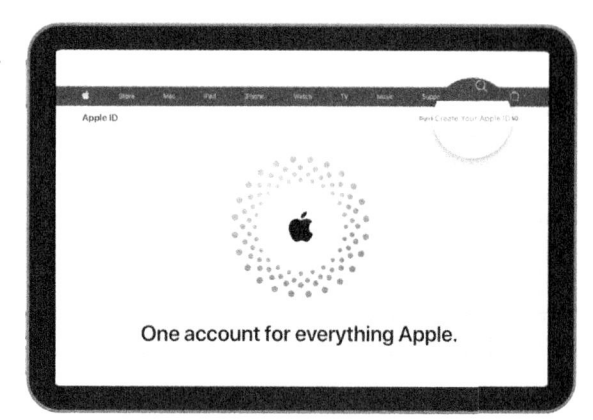

4. **Enter Your Information**:
   - You'll be prompted to enter your first and last name, date of birth, and email address. If you don't have an email address, you can create a free one through Apple.

5. **Set a Password**:
   - Choose a strong password that's easy for you to remember but hard for others to guess.
   - Apple requires passwords with at least eight characters, including a number and an uppercase letter.

6. **Answer Security Questions**:
   - These questions help you recover your account if you forget your password. Choose answers you can easily recall.

7. **Agree to the Terms and Conditions**:
   - Read through the terms (or skim if you prefer) and tap Agree.

8. **Verify Your Account**:
   - Apple will send a verification email to the address you provided. Open the email on any device and click the verification link.

Once verified, you're ready to start using your Apple ID on your iPad.

Signing In to Your Apple ID

If you already have an Apple ID, sign in to link it to your iPad:

1. Open the **Settings** app.

2. Tap **Sign In to Your iPad** at the top of the menu.

3. Enter your Apple ID email address and password.

4. Follow any additional prompts, such as entering a verification code sent to your trusted device.

Once signed in, your iPad will automatically sync with your Apple ID.

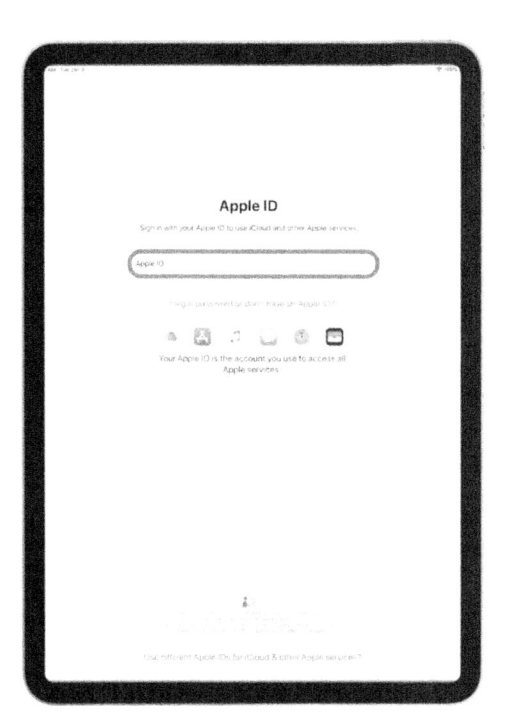

Managing Your Apple ID

Your Apple ID isn't something you set and forget. Regular management ensures smooth operation and security.

Updating Personal Information

1. Open **Settings** and tap your name at the top of the menu.

2. Select **Name, Phone Numbers, and Email** to update your contact details.

3. Make changes as needed and tap **Save**.

Managing Payment Methods

Your Apple ID is necessary to make purchases on the App Store and iTunes. To update your payment methods:

1. In the Settings app, tap your name and select **Payment & Shipping**.

2. Add, update, or remove payment methods as necessary.

Changing Your Password

If you suspect your Apple ID password has been compromised, change it immediately:

1. Open **Settings** and tap your name.
2. Select **Password & Security > Change Password**.
3. Follow the on-screen instructions to create a new password.

Two-Factor Authentication

Enable two-factor authentication (2FA) for added security. This requires a trusted device or phone number to verify your identity when signing in. To enable 2FA:

1. Go to **Settings, tap your name, and then choose Password & Security**.
2. Turn on the **Two-Factor Authentication** and follow the prompts.

Troubleshooting Apple ID Issues

Forgot Your Password?

1. Go to **Settings** and tap your name.
2. Select **Password & Security > Change Password**.
3. Tap **Forgot Password?** and follow the recovery steps.

Apple ID Locked?

Your account may be locked for security reasons if there are too many failed login attempts. To unlock it:

1. Visit iforgot.apple.com.
2. Follow the instructions to verify your identity and reset your password.

Email Not Received for Verification?

1. Check your spam or junk folder.//
2. Ensure the email address you provided is correct.
3. Resend the verification email from the Apple ID settings page.

Tips for Apple ID Security

- **Use a Strong Password**: Avoid easily guessed passwords like "123456" or "password."
- **Enable Two-Factor Authentication**: This adds an extra layer of security.
- **Be Wary of Phishing Scams**: Apple will never ask for your password or verification code via email.
- **Keep Your Recovery Information Up to Date**: Regularly review and update your trusted phone numbers and backup email addresses.

By setting up and managing your Apple ID, you're creating a secure gateway to Apple's vast ecosystem of tools and services. With your account in place, you're ready to explore the App Store, use iCloud for backups, and connect with loved ones via FaceTime.

Sending and Receiving Emails Like a Pro

Email remains one of the easiest and most reliable ways to communicate. With your iPad, managing email becomes a seamless process, whether you're staying in touch with loved ones, receiving important updates, or subscribing to your favorite newsletters. In this sub-chapter, we'll explore how to set up email accounts, compose and organize messages, and use built-in tools to simplify your experience.

Setting Up Your Email Account

Before you can start sending or receiving emails, you need to add your email account to the Mail app. Here's how:

- iPad Seniors Guide -

1. **Open Settings:**

   o Tap the Settings app on your Home Screen.

2. **Select 'Mail' from the Menu:**

   o Scroll down and tap Mail, then select Accounts.

3. **Add an Account:**

   o Tap Add Account and choose your email provider (e.g., Gmail, Yahoo, Outlook, or iCloud). If your provider isn't listed, tap Other.

4. **Enter Your Email Details:**

   o Type in your email address and password. If required, input additional details, such as incoming and outgoing mail server settings (your email provider can help with this).

5. **Confirm Setup:**

   o Tap Next and wait for the iPad to verify your account. Once verified, select what you'd like to sync (Mail, Contacts, Calendars, etc.) and tap Save.

Your email account is now ready to use in the Mail app.

Navigating the Mail App

Once your account is set up, the Mail app becomes your hub for email communication. Here's a breakdown of its main features:

Inbox View

- Open the Mail app to see your inbox.

- Emails are listed by date, with the newest messages at the top. Unread messages are indicated by a blue dot.

Folders

- Access folders like Sent, Trash, Drafts, and any custom folders you've created. Tap Mailboxes in the upper-left corner to switch between accounts or folders.

Search

- Use the Search bar at the top of the inbox to quickly find emails by sender, subject, or keyword.

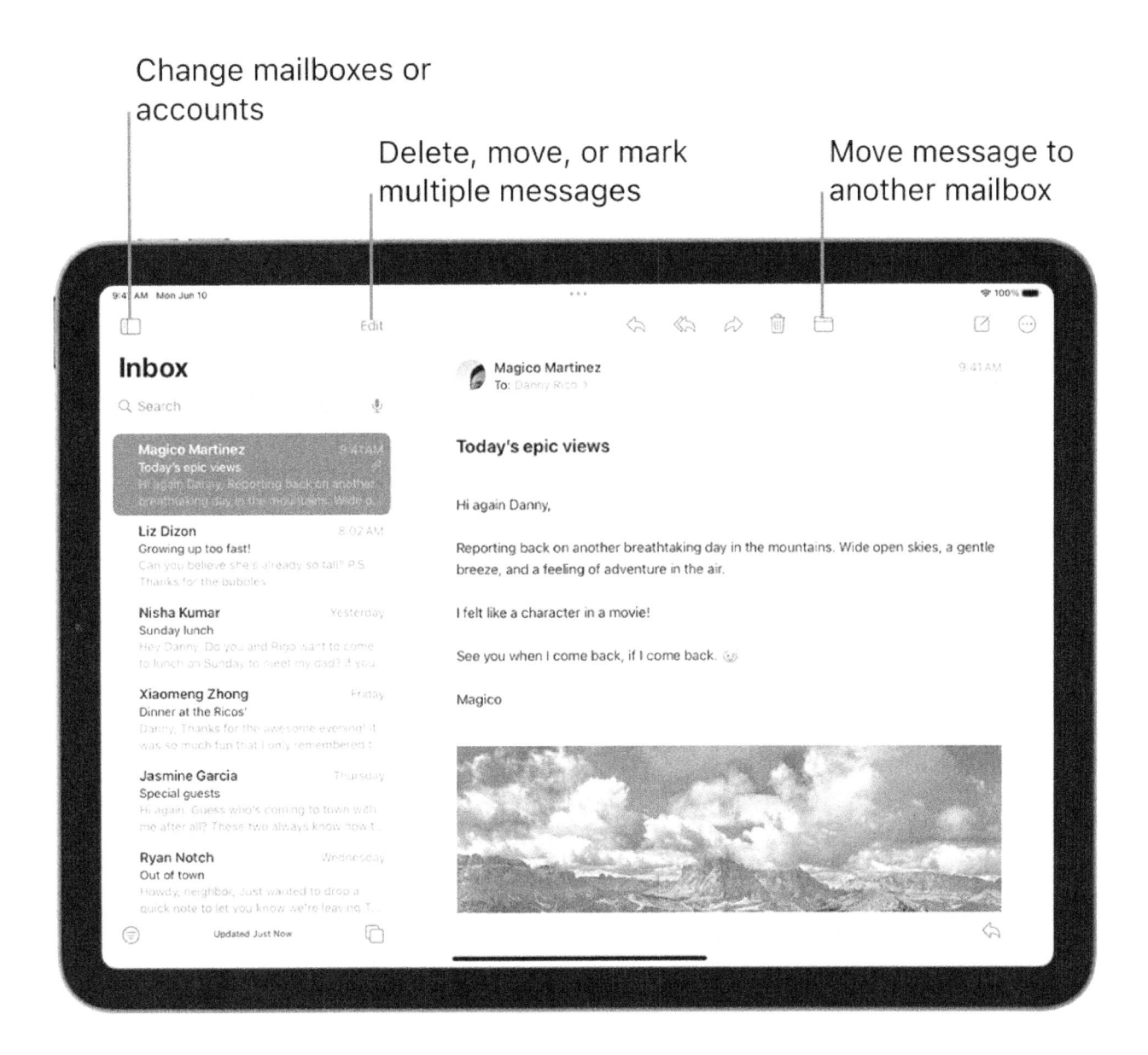

Change mailboxes or accounts

Delete, move, or mark multiple messages

Move message to another mailbox

Swipe Gestures

- Swipe left on an email for options like **Delete or Archive**.
- To mark an email as read or unread, swipe right on it.

Composing and Sending Emails

Crafting a professional and effective email is easy with your iPad. Follow these steps to send messages like a pro:

How to Compose an Email

1. **Tap the Compose Icon**:
    - In the Mail app, tap the square with a pencil icon in the bottom-right corner.

2. **Add a Recipient**:
    - Type the recipient's email address in the To field. If you've emailed them before, their address may auto-complete as you type.

3. **Write a Subject Line**:
    - Keep it brief but informative. For example, "Photos from the Family Reunion" or "Questions About Tomorrow's Meeting."

4. **Compose Your Message**:
    - Tap the blank space below the subject line to write your email. The on-screen keyboard will appear for typing.

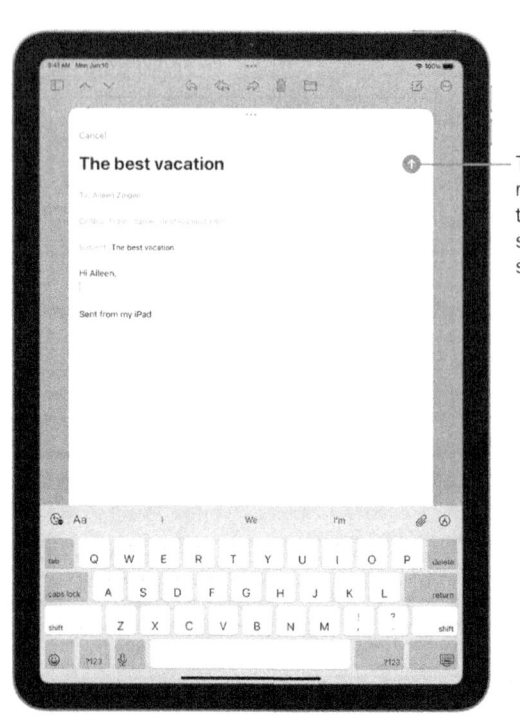

Tap to send the message, or touch and hold to schedule a time to send it later.

5. **Attach Files or Photos**:

    ○ Tap the paper clip or camera icon above the keyboard to attach photos, documents, or other files.

6. **Send Your Email**:

    ○ When you're done, tap the blue arrow icon in the top-right corner to send your message.

Pro Tip: If you're not ready to send an email, tap Cancel and select Save Draft to return to it later.

Receiving and Managing Emails

Staying on top of your inbox is simple with these strategies:

Reading Emails

- Tap any email in your inbox to open and read it.
- Embedded links, attachments, and images are often clickable, allowing you to explore additional content.

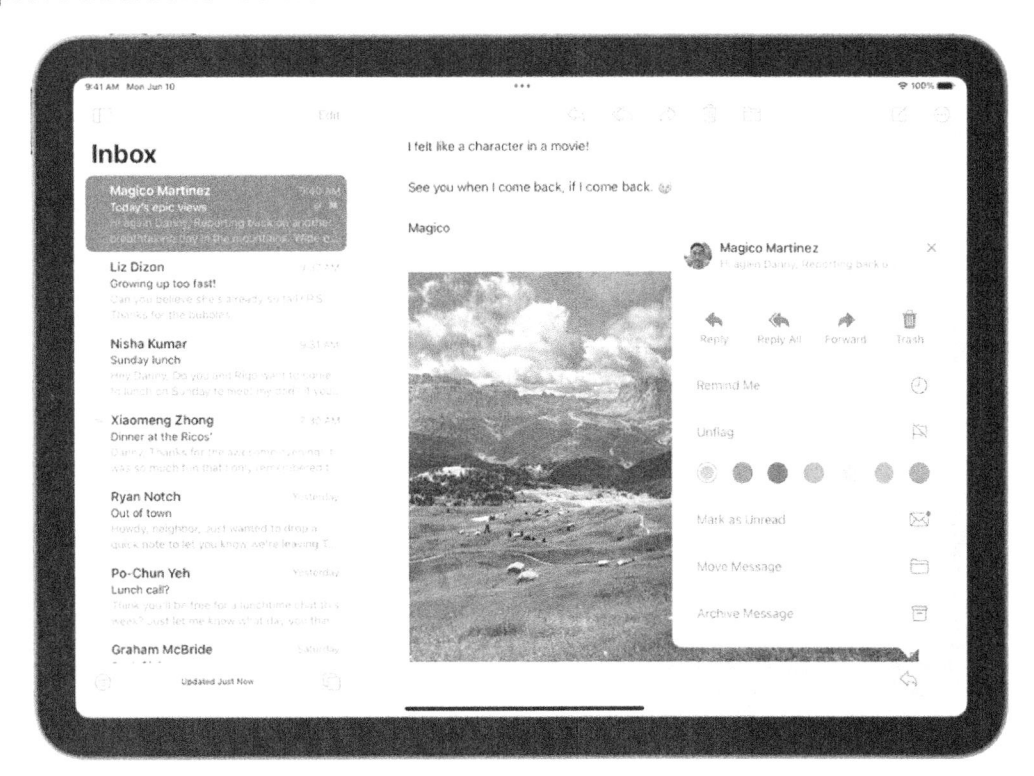

Replying to Emails

- Tap the **Reply** icon (a curved arrow) at the bottom of the message. Choose Reply to respond to the sender or **Reply All** if multiple recipients are involved.

Forwarding Emails

- To share an email with someone else, tap the **Reply icon** and select **Forward.** Add the recipient's address and include a personal note if needed.

Deleting Emails

- To delete an email from your inbox, swipe left on the email and then tap "Delete". Deleted messages are moved to the Trash folder, where they can be recovered for a limited time.

Using Advanced Email Features

Take your email skills to the next level with these built-in tools:

Organizing Emails with Folders

- Create folders to keep your inbox tidy. For example, you can create folders for family emails, work messages, or important documents.

- To create a folder, tap Mailboxes > Edit > New Mailbox, name your folder, and assign it to an account.

Flagging Important Emails

- Tap the **Flag icon** while viewing an email to mark it for easy reference. Flags appear as brightly colored indicators in your inbox.

Using VIP Contacts

- Add frequent contacts to your **VIP** list for quick access. Their emails will appear in a dedicated **VIP** inbox. To add a **VIP**, tap the sender's name and select Add to **VIP**.

Scheduling Emails

- While composing an email, press and hold the **Send button** to schedule the message for a later time.

Troubleshooting Email Issues

Can't Send or Receive Emails?

- Ensure your iPad is connected to Wi-Fi.
- Verify your email account settings in **Settings > Mail > Accounts**.

Emails Not Syncing?

- Go to **Settings > Mail > Accounts** and ensure the account's sync options are enabled.
- To restart your iPad, press and hold the Power button, then select "Restart" from the menu.

Accidentally Deleted an Email?

- Check the **Trash folder.** Tap the email and select **Move** to restore it to your inbox.

Tips for a Stress-Free Email Experience

- **Make sure to check your spam folder**: As legitimate emails can sometimes be mistakenly sent there.
- **Unsubscribe from Unwanted Newsletters**: Save time by reducing inbox clutter. Look for the Unsubscribe link at the bottom of unwanted emails.
- **Set Notifications Wisely**: Customize email notifications in **Settings > Notifications > Mail** to avoid being overwhelmed.

By mastering the Mail app, you'll find it easy to send and receive emails confidently. Whether you're catching up with loved ones or handling day-to-day tasks, email on your iPad can keep you connected and organized.

Essential Apps and Their Uses

Exploring Pre-installed Apps: Safari, Mail, and Photos

The iPad comes equipped with a variety of pre-installed apps designed to make your digital experience seamless and efficient. These essential apps cover key areas like web browsing, communication, and photo management. In this sub-chapter, we'll dive into three of the most important apps you'll use daily: **Safari, Mail,** and **Photos.** We'll explore how to use them, customize settings, and get the most out of these built-in tools.

Safari: Your Gateway to the Web

Safari is the default web browser on your iPad, and it's a powerful tool for browsing the internet. Whether you're researching a topic, reading the news, or checking your favorite websites, Safari is designed to make your online experience smooth and intuitive.

Navigating the Web

1. **Open Safari**:
    - Find the Safari icon on your Home Screen and tap on it to open the browser.

2. **Search or Enter a URL**:
    - At the top of the screen, you'll see a combined address and search bar. You can type in a website URL directly (e.g., www.apple.com) or enter a search term to find relevant websites.

3. **Accessing Bookmarks and History**:
   - Tap the book icon in the bottom menu to access your bookmarks. You can save your favorite websites here for easy access.
   - Tap the clock icon to view your browsing history. This is helpful if you need to find a website you visited recently.

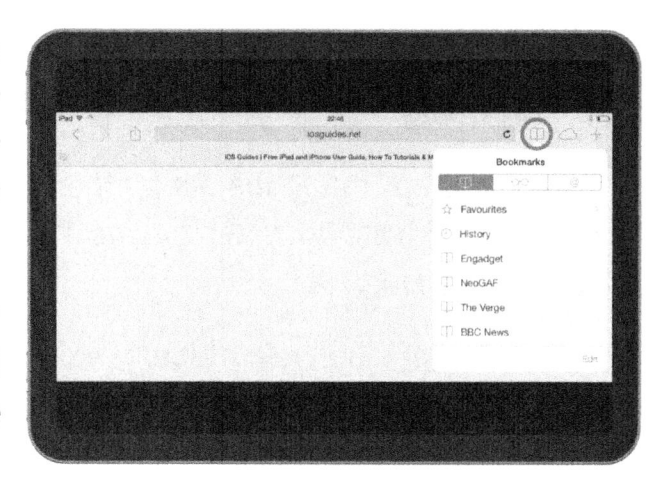

Using Tabs for Multiple Websites

- Safari allows you to open multiple web pages at once using **tabs**. To open a new tab:

   1. Tap the **tab icon** in the upper-right corner (it looks like two overlapping squares).

   2. Select the **+** icon to open a new tab.

   3. To switch between tabs, tap the one you want to view.

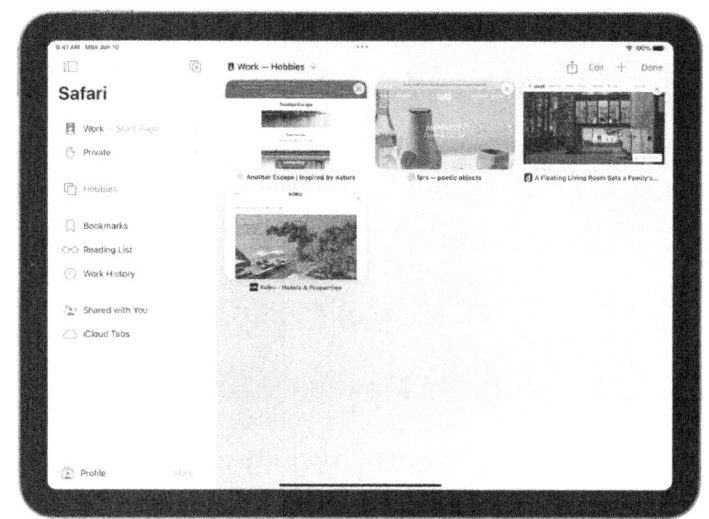

Private Browsing Mode

- If you want to browse without saving your history or cookies, you can use **Private Browsing**:

    1. Tap the **Tabs** icon, then select **Private** to enter private browsing mode.

    2. Your browsing history will not be saved, and any websites you visit will not appear in your search suggestions.

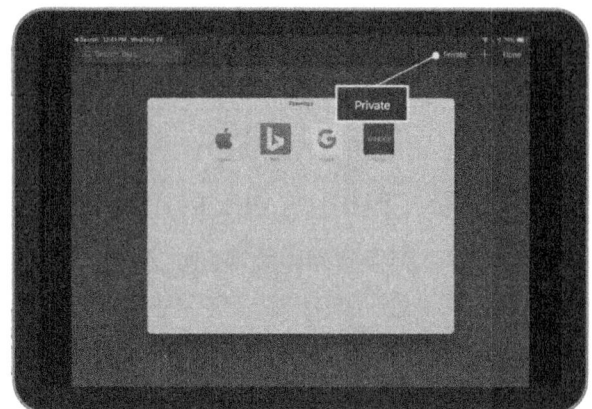

Mail: Organizing and Managing Your Emails

Mail is the app you'll use to manage your email accounts on your iPad. It integrates with various email providers, such as Gmail, Yahoo, iCloud, and more. Whether you're sending, reading, or organizing emails, Mail makes it easy to stay connected.

Navigating Your Inbox

1. **Open Mail**:

    - Tap the Mail icon on your Home Screen to open the app.

2. **Viewing and Managing Emails**:

    - Your inbox will appear first, with the most recent messages at the top.

    - Tap any email to read it.

    - Swipe left on any email to delete or archive it.

3. **Organizing Your Emails**:

    - Use **Folders** to categorize your messages (e.g., "Work," "Family," or "Newsletters"). To create a new folder:

1. Tap **Mailboxes** in the upper-left corner.
2. Tap **Edit**, then **New Mailbox**. Name your folder and tap **Save**.

Composing and Sending Emails

1. Tap the **Compose** icon (a pencil in a square) to create a new message.
2. In the **To** field, enter the recipient's email address. Add a **Subject** and write your message.
3. Tap the **Send** button when you're ready.

Using Attachments

- You can attach photos, documents, and other files to your email. When composing a message, tap the **paperclip** icon or **photo icon** to attach items from your iPad.

Photos: Capturing and Organizing Memories

The **Photos** app on your iPad is your digital photo album. It allows you to take pictures, store them, and organize them for easy access. The app also comes with powerful editing tools to enhance your photos, and it integrates with iCloud for backup and syncing across all your Apple devices.

Viewing Your Photos

1. **Open Photos:**
    - Tap the **Photos app i**con to open your photo library.

2. **Browse Through Albums**:

   - Photos are automatically sorted into albums such as **Recents, Favorites,** and **Selfies.**

   - To view a specific album, tap on it to open it.

3. **Using the Search Function**:

   - To quickly find a photo, tap the Search tab at the bottom, then type a keyword (e.g., "vacation" or "dog").

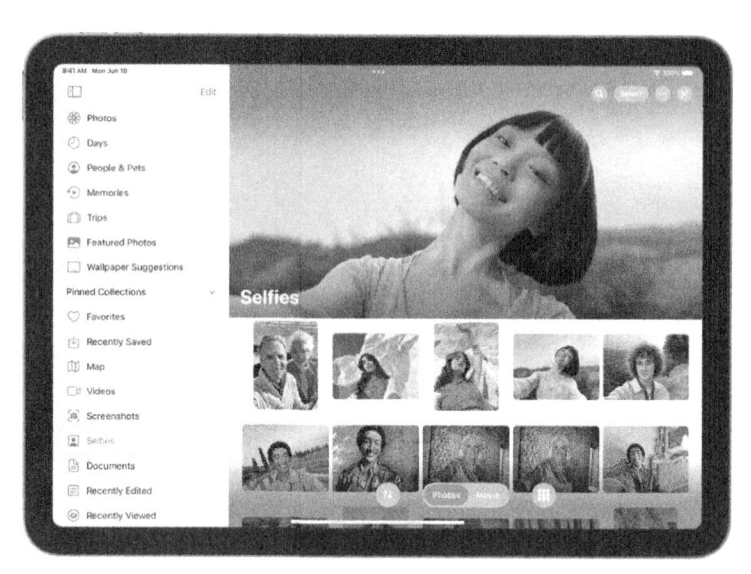

Editing Photos

- The **Photos app** comes with a range of editing tools to enhance your pictures:

   1. Tap on any photo to view it.

   2. Tap **Edit** in the upper-right corner.

   3. Adjust elements like brightness, contrast, and sharpness using the available sliders.

   4. Use the **filters** and **crop tools** to refine your photo further.

   5. When finished, tap Done to save your edits.

Creating Albums and Organizing Photos

- To organize your photos into albums:

1. Tap **Albums** in the lower-right corner.

2. Select **+** to create a new album. Name it and add photos by selecting them from your library.

Safari, Mail, and Photos are three of the most essential pre-installed apps that will become your go-to tools on the iPad. With Safari, you can easily browse the web; with Mail, you'll stay connected through email; and with Photos, you can capture and organize memories. These apps offer a solid foundation for getting the most out of your iPad, and as you become more familiar with them, you will discover methods to enhance your daily life, making it more efficient and enjoyable.

Downloading and Organizing New Apps from the App Store

Exploring the App Store

The **App Store** is the hub for all your app needs. Here's how you can access it and begin your journey to discovering new apps:

1. **Opening the App Store**:

    - Find and tap the App Store icon on your iPad's Home Screen. The icon looks like a blue circle with a white "A" formed from paintbrushes.

2. **Navigating the App Store**:

    - At the bottom of the App Store, you'll see tabs such as Today, Games, Apps, Arcade, and Search.

    - Tap Today to find daily app recommendations and highlights.

- *iPad Seniors Guide* -

- Tap Apps to browse categories like Health & Fitness, News, Education, and more.

- If you're searching for a specific app, tap Search and type the name of the app you're looking for. You can also search for app categories or types.

3. **Reading App Details**:

   - When you find an app you're interested in, tap on it to open its page. Here, you'll see:

     - A description of the app's features and capabilities.

     - Screenshots or videos showing what the app looks like in use.

     - Reviews and ratings from other users.

     - Information on whether the app is free or requires a purchase or subscription.

Downloading and Installing Apps

Once you've found an app you want to try, downloading and installing it is quick and easy. Here's how to do it:

1. **Tapping the Download Button**:

   - On an app's page, you'll see either a Get button (for free apps) or a Price button (for paid apps).

   - If the app is free, simply tap Get. If it's paid, tap the price and follow the prompts to complete the purchase.

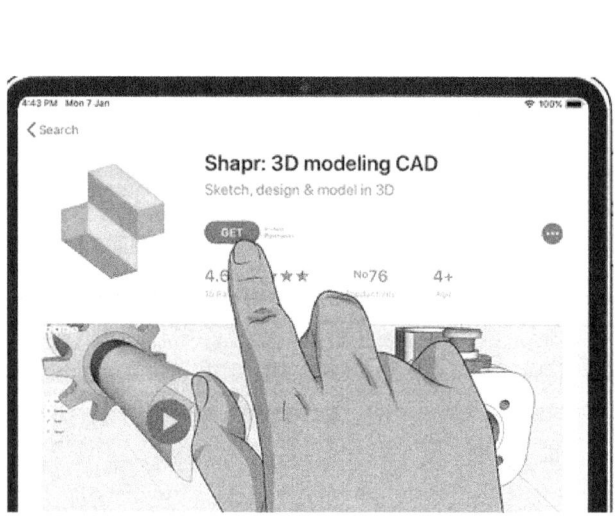

2. **Using Face ID or Apple ID Password**:

    ○ If you have Face ID or Touch ID enabled, the iPad will prompt you to confirm the download using your face or fingerprint.

    ○ If you don't have Face ID or Touch ID set up, you'll need to enter your Apple ID password to authorize the download.

3. **Waiting for the App to Install**:

    ○ Once confirmed, the app will begin downloading. You'll see a progress circle in place of the Get or price button, and the app will automatically install on your Home Screen when it's done.

    ○ You can monitor the progress by looking at the app's icon, which will slowly fill with color as the download completes.

Organizing Your Apps

As you begin downloading more apps, it's important to keep your Home Screen organized so you can quickly find the apps you use most often. Here's how to manage your app layout:

Arranging Apps on the Home Screen

1. **Moving Apps**:

    ○ To move an app, press and hold its icon until it starts to jiggle.

- *iPad Seniors Guide* -

- To move the app icon, simply drag it to your preferred location on the screen or even to a different page.
- Tap Done in the top-right corner to stop the icons from jiggling once you're finished.

2. **Creating Folders:**
    - If you have multiple apps that are related (e.g., all your fitness apps or all your games), you can group them into folders to keep your iPad organized.
    - To create a folder, press and hold an app until it starts to jiggle.
    - Drag the app on top of another app that you'd like to group it with. The iPad will automatically create a folder for them. You can then rename the folder by tapping on the folder name at the top of the group.
    - Tap Done when you're finished organizing.

3. **Using the App Library (iPadOS 14 and later):**
    - With iPadOS 14 and newer, Apple unveiled the App Library, a feature that automatically organizes your apps into categories and makes it easy to find apps without cluttering your Home Screen.

- To access the App Library, swipe to the last page of your Home Screen or swipe down on your Home Screen to search.

- In the App Library, apps are grouped into categories such as Recently Added, Productivity, Social, and more. You can also search for specific apps using the search bar at the top.

Updating and Managing Your Apps

Just as it's important to download apps, it's also essential to keep them up to date for the best performance and security.

1. **Updating Apps**:

    - Open the App Store and tap on your profile icon in the upper-right corner.

    - Under Available Updates, you'll see a list of apps that have updates waiting. Tap Update All to update all your apps at once, or tap Update next to individual apps.

    - Keeping your apps updated ensures you get the latest features and security fixes.

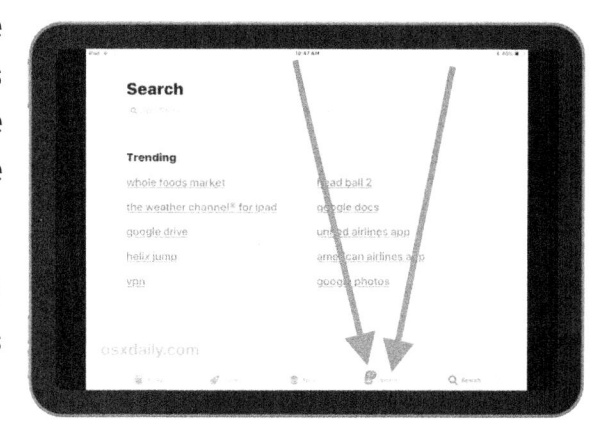

2. **Managing App Notifications**:

    - Some apps will send notifications to alert you about new content, messages, or reminders. If you want to customize these notifications:

        1. Go to Settings > Notifications.

        2. Scroll down and tap on the app you want to adjust.

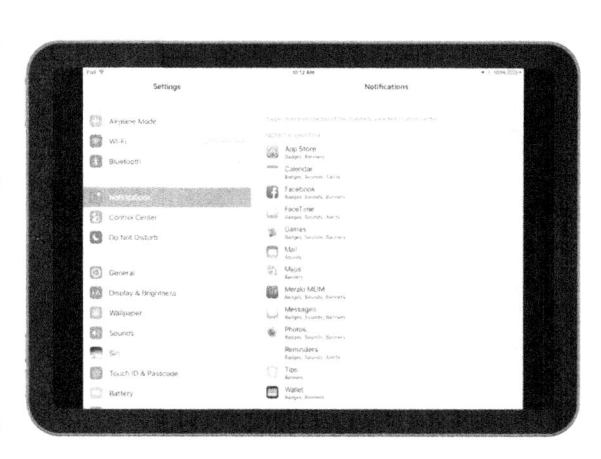

3. Here, you can turn notifications on or off and choose how they appear (e.g., on the Lock Screen, as banners, etc.).

3. **Deleting Apps You No Longer Need**:
    - To delete an app, press and hold its icon on the Home Screen.
    - When the icons start to jiggle, tap the X icon on the app you wish to remove.
    - Confirm by tapping Delete. The app will be uninstalled from your iPad, which will free up storage space.

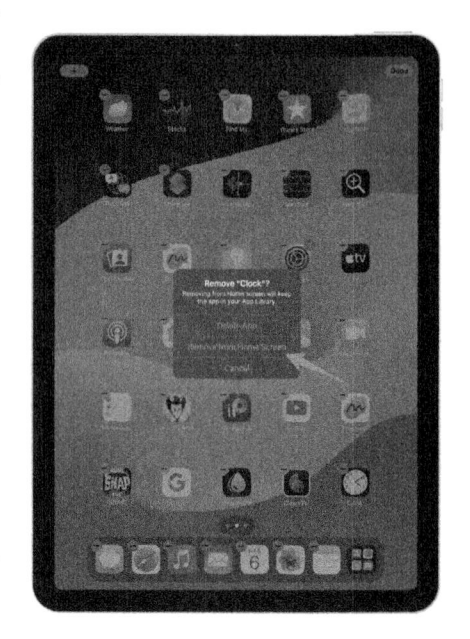

Downloading and organizing apps is one of the first things you'll want to do when setting up your iPad. The App Store offers an endless array of apps that suit all kinds of needs, from productivity and entertainment to creativity and health. By organizing your apps into folders and keeping them up to date, you can ensure your iPad remains efficient and easy to navigate.

Managing Storage and Deleting Apps You Don't Need

One of the most important aspects of maintaining your iPad's performance is managing storage. Over time, as you download apps, take photos, and save files, your iPad's storage can fill up. If you notice that your device is slowing down or that you're running out of space, it may be time to manage your apps and data. In this sub-chapter, we'll guide you through managing your storage and removing apps you no longer need, all while making sure your iPad continues to run smoothly.

Understanding Your iPad's Storage

Before we dive into how to manage your apps and data, it's helpful to know how much storage you have available and what's taking up space.

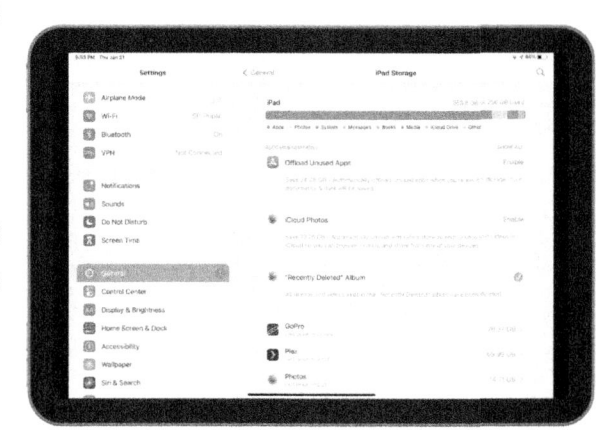

1. **Checking Available Storage**:
   To see how much storage is available on your iPad:

   - Open Settings.

   - Scroll down and tap General.

   - Tap iPad Storage.

   - Here, you'll see a visual representation of your storage, with categories like Apps, Photos, Media, and System, showing how much space each section is using.

   - If you're nearing your storage limit, it's a good idea to review the apps and data that are taking up the most space.

2. **Breaking Down Storage Usage**:
   Under iPad Storage, you'll see a list of your apps, sorted by the amount of space they use. The apps that take up the most space will be at the top. Tapping on any app will show more details, including how much storage the app itself uses, along with any data associated with it (e.g., documents, photos, or videos).

Deleting Apps You Don't Use Anymore

If you're running low on storage, the most effective way to free up space is to delete apps you no longer use. Here's how you can remove them:

1. **From the Home Screen**:

   - Press and hold the app icon you want to delete.

   - Once the icons begin to jiggle, tap the X in the upper-left corner of the app icon.

   - A confirmation prompt will appear asking you to delete the app. Tap "Delete" to remove it from your iPad.

2. **From the Settings Menu**:

    - Open Settings and tap General.

    - Select iPad Storage and scroll down the list of apps.

    - Choose the app you want to remove, then tap on "Delete App". To confirm your decision, tap "Delete App" once more in the pop-up window.

3. **Offloading Unused Apps**:
    If you don't want to completely delete an app but need to free up space, you can use the Offload Unused Apps feature. This removes the app from your device. However, it retains its data, allowing you to reinstall it later without losing your settings or information.

    - Go to **Settings > General > iPad Storage**.

    - Tap on an app you rarely use and select **Offload App**.

    - The app will be removed, but its documents and data will remain on your device. When you decide to reinstall it, everything will be restored.

Managing Large Files and Data

It's not just apps that can take up a lot of space—photos, videos, and other media files can also fill your iPad quickly. Here's how you can manage these files to free up some storage:

1. **Managing Photos and Videos**:
    Photos and videos often consume the most storage. To manage them:

    - Open the **Photos app** and go through your albums. Delete any photos or videos that are unnecessary.

    - Tap the **Trash icon** to delete, then go to the **Recently Deleted** album and select **Delete All** to permanently remove them.

- o If you want to store photos without taking up space on your iPad, you can use iCloud to store them in the cloud. This way, they're accessible from any device without using your device's storage.

2. **Managing Music and Movies**:
   If you've downloaded music, movies, or shows to your iPad, these files can take up significant space. To manage them:

   - o Open the Music app or TV app, depending on where your media is stored.

   - o Review your downloads and remove any content you no longer need.

   - o If you use Apple Music or Apple TV+, you can stream content without downloading it, saving storage space.

3. **Documents and Other Files**:
   Files such as PDFs, Word documents, and other downloaded content can also take up a significant amount of storage. To manage these:

   - o Open the Files app, where you can find all your documents, and go through them to delete anything you no longer need.

   - o You can also move files to cloud storage services like iCloud Drive or Google Drive to free up space on your iPad.

Using iCloud to Free Up Storage

iCloud is Apple's cloud storage service that allows you to back up your data, including photos, documents, and apps. Using iCloud, you can free up space on your iPad by storing your data remotely while keeping it accessible whenever you need it.

1. **Backing Up to iCloud**:
   To ensure your data is backed up, go to Settings > [Your Name] > iCloud > iCloud Backup and turn on iCloud Backup. Tap Back Up Now to start a manual backup.

2. **Using iCloud for Photos and Documents**:
   If you want to store your photos and videos in iCloud, open

Settings, tap **[Your Name] > iCloud, and enable iCloud Photos**. This will store your photos and videos securely. In the cloud, free up space on your device. Similarly, you can use iCloud Drive for documents, making them accessible from any device without taking up storage on your iPad.

Managing your iPad's storage is essential for maintaining its performance and ensuring you have enough space for the apps and files you use most. By regularly checking your available storage, deleting unused apps, and organizing your media, you can keep your iPad running smoothly and efficiently. Additionally, using iCloud to back up and store files remotely can help free up space on your device.

Keeping in Touch with Loved Ones

Video Calls Made Simple: Using FaceTime

Keeping in touch with loved ones has never been easier, thanks to FaceTime, Apple's built-in video and audio calling app. Whether you want to see your grandchildren, chat with friends, or catch up with distant family members, FaceTime allows you to share moments with them in real time, no matter where they are. This sub-chapter will guide you through everything you need to know to start making video calls with confidence.

What Is FaceTime and Why Use It?

FaceTime is a free app that comes pre-installed on every iPad. It uses your device's camera and microphone to enable high-quality video and audio calls over Wi-Fi or cellular data. Unlike traditional phone calls, FaceTime offers a face-to-face connection, bringing warmth and clarity to your conversations.

Why choose FaceTime?

- **User-Friendly**: Its intuitive design makes it accessible, even for beginners.
- **Cost-Effective**: FaceTime calls are free as long as you're connected to Wi-Fi.
- **Versatile**: Use it for one-on-one chats or group calls with up to 32 participants.

Setting Up FaceTime

Before you start making video calls, it's important to ensure FaceTime is properly set up on your iPad.

1. **Sign In with Your Apple ID**:
    - Open the **Settings** app.
    - Scroll down and tap **FaceTime**.
    - Ensure FaceTime is turned on (the switch should be green).

- o If prompted, sign in with your Apple ID. This connects FaceTime to your email address and phone number (if applicable), allowing others to contact you.

2. **Customize Your Settings**:

    - o Under the FaceTime settings, you can choose how people can reach you. For example, you can use your email address or phone number.
    - o You can also set a **Caller ID**, which determines what others see when you call them.

3. **Ensure Camera and Microphone Permissions Are Enabled**:

    - o To check, go to **Settings > Privacy & Security > Camera** and ensure FaceTime is enabled.
    - o Repeat this process under **Microphone** to confirm FaceTime has access.

Making a Video Call with FaceTime

Once your FaceTime is set up, you're ready to make your first call. Here's how:

1. **Open the FaceTime App**:

    - o Open the **FaceTime** app by tapping its icon on your Home Screen.

2. **Start a New Call**:

    - o Tap the + button in the upper-right corner.
    - o Enter the email address or phone number of the person you wish to contact.. If they're already in your Contacts, start typing their name and select it from the suggestions.

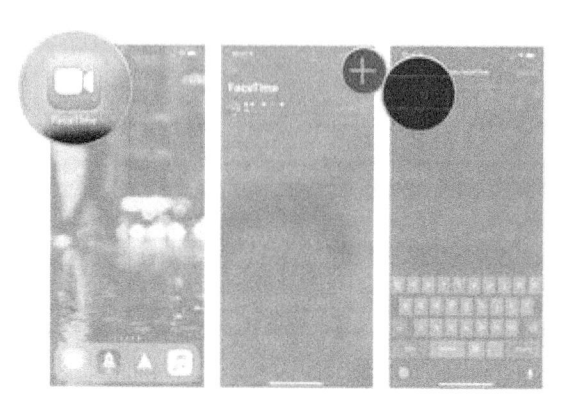

3. **Choose the Call Type**:

    o Tap Video to make a video call.

    o If you prefer an audio-only call, tap **Audio** instead.

4. **Wait for the Connection**:

    o Once you initiate the call, your iPad will attempt to connect with the recipient. When they answer, you'll see their face on your screen and hear their voice.

Using FaceTime Features During a Call

FaceTime offers several features to enhance your video calling experience.

1. **Switch Between Cameras**:

    o Tap the camera icon to switch between the front-facing and rear-facing cameras. This is helpful if you want to show something around you.

2. **Mute Yourself**:

    o Press the microphone icon to mute your audio if you need to momentarily stop others from hearing you.

3. **Use Picture-in-Picture Mode**:

    o To return to the home screen, press the Home button (or swipe up from the bottom of the screen if your iPad lacks a Home button) during a FaceTime call. The call will shrink into a small window, allowing you to multitask on your iPad while continuing the conversation.

4. **Add More Participants**:
    - Tap the **+ Add People** button to invite others to join your call. This is perfect for family catch-ups or virtual group meetings.

Receiving and Answering Calls

You don't always have to initiate calls—sometimes, friends and family will call you! Here's how to answer:

1. **When a FaceTime Call Comes In**:
    - A notification will appear on your screen with options to **Accept** or **Decline**.
    - Tap **Accept** to answer the call.

2. **If You Miss a Call**:
    - Open the **FaceTime** app and tap the **Recents** tab to see a list of missed calls. From here, you can tap on a name or number to call them back.

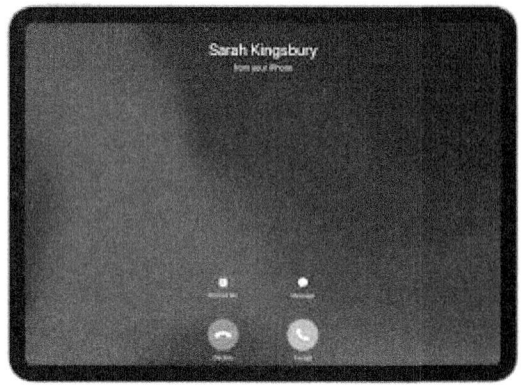

Troubleshooting Common Issues

FaceTime is designed to work seamlessly, but occasionally, you may encounter issues. Here's how to address them:

1. **Poor Video or Audio Quality**:
    - Ensure you're connected to a strong Wi-Fi signal.
    - Ask the other person to check their connection as well.

2. **Can't Make or Receive Calls**:
    - Verify that FaceTime is enabled in **Settings**.
    - Check your internet connection and restart your iPad if needed.

3. **The Other Person Isn't Answering**:

    o Confirm their contact details are correct and that they're available to receive FaceTime calls.

FaceTime is an effective tool for keeping in touch with loved ones, offering a way to share smiles, stories, and moments even from afar. With a few simple steps, you can easily set up and start using FaceTime to make video calls. By exploring its features and addressing any challenges, you'll become a pro in no time.

Staying Social with Messages and WhatsApp

In today's digital world, staying in touch with loved ones doesn't have to be complicated. Your iPad provides two powerful tools for communication: **Messages** and **WhatsApp**. Whether you prefer text messages, group chats, or sharing photos and videos, these apps make it easy to stay connected, no matter where your friends and family are. This sub-chapter will guide you through using both apps effectively so you can keep the conversation flowing.

Using the Messages App

The **Messages** app, pre-installed on your iPad, is a versatile tool for sending text messages, photos, videos, and more. It works seamlessly with other Apple devices, making it the go-to choice for connecting with anyone in the Apple ecosystem.

Getting Started with Messages

1. **Opening the App**:

    o Tap the **Messages** app icon on your Home Screen.

    o If this is your first time using it, you'll be prompted to sign in with your Apple ID.

2. **Starting a New Conversation**:

    o Tap the **Compose** button (a square with a pencil) in the upper-right corner.

- o In the "To" field, type the recipient's phone number, email address, or name (if they're in your Contacts).

3. **Sending a Message**:

    - o Type your message in the text box at the bottom of the screen.
    - o Tap the **Send** button (a blue arrow) to send your message.

Adding a Personal Touch

- **Share Photos and Videos**: Tap the camera icon to take a new photo or choose one from your library.

- **Use Stickers and Emojis**: Tap the smiley face icon to add fun stickers, emojis, or GIFs to your messages.

- **Send Voice Notes**: Hold the microphone icon to record and send a quick voice message.

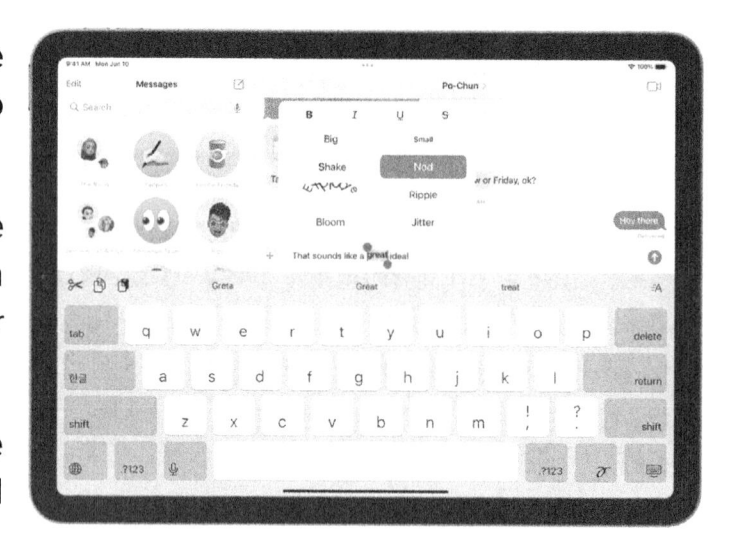

Group Messaging Made Simple

- To initiate a group chat, add multiple recipients in the "To" field.

- Give the group a name by tapping the group icon at the top and selecting **Change Name and Photo**.

- Share updates, photos, and links with everyone in the group simultaneously.

Connecting Through WhatsApp

If some of your loved ones don't use Apple devices, **WhatsApp** is a fantastic alternative. This popular messaging app works across platforms, allowing you to communicate with Android and Windows users, too.

Installing WhatsApp on Your iPad

WhatsApp doesn't have a dedicated iPad app, but you can still use it by accessing WhatsApp Web or downloading a third-party app.

1. **Accessing WhatsApp Web:**
    - Open the **Safari** browser on your iPad.
    - Go to **web.whatsapp.com**.
    - On your phone, open WhatsApp and tap **Settings > Linked Devices > Link a Device**.
    - Scan the QR code displayed on your iPad to link your account.
2. **Using Third-Party Apps:**
    - Visit the App Store and search for a WhatsApp companion app, such as "Messenger for WhatsApp."
    - Download and follow the app's instructions to set up WhatsApp on your iPad.

Features to Explore in WhatsApp

- **Chats**: Send text messages, photos, and videos to individuals or groups.

- **Voice and Video Calls**: Tap the phone or video camera icon to call your contacts directly from WhatsApp.

- **Status Updates**: Share short updates, photos, or videos that disappear after 24 hours.

Managing Notifications

- Ensure you don't miss important messages by enabling notifications.

    - Go to **Settings > Notifications > WhatsApp** and toggle notifications on.

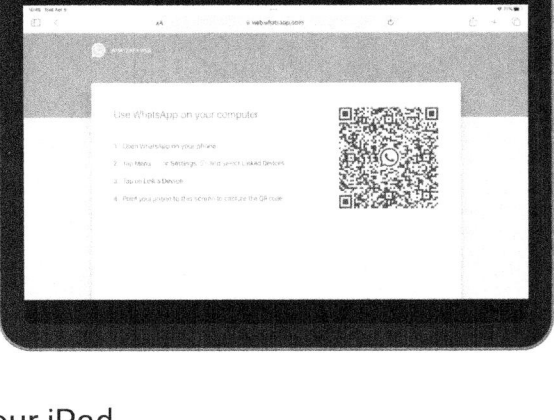

Tips for Staying Connected Safely

Whether you're using Messages or WhatsApp, staying connected online requires a few simple precautions:

1. **Protect Your Privacy**:
    - In Messages, avoid sharing sensitive information like passwords.
    - In WhatsApp, customize your privacy settings by going to Settings > Privacy to control who can see your profile photo and status.

2. **Beware of Spam**:
    - If you receive messages from unknown contacts, don't click on suspicious links. Block and report such contacts to avoid scams.

3. **Keep Apps Updated**:
    - Regularly update Messages and WhatsApp to ensure you have the latest security features and improvements.

Messages and WhatsApp make it easier than ever to stay connected with loved ones. With just a few taps, you can share memories, exchange ideas, and strengthen your relationships, no matter the distance.

Sharing Photos and Files Easily

Your iPad makes sharing photos and files with loved ones a breeze. Whether you want to send cherished memories or important documents, the tools available on your device are simple, intuitive, and incredibly versatile. This sub-chapter will guide you step-by-step through the process of sharing photos, videos, and files using various methods so you can stay connected and organized.

Sharing Photos with the Photos App

The **Photos** app is the central hub for managing and sharing your favorite snapshots.

Sending a Single Photo

1. **Open the Photos App**:

    - Tap the **Photos** icon on your Home Screen.

    - Browse your library or use the search bar to find the photo you want to share.

2. **Select the Photo**:

    - Tap on the photo to open it.

    - Look for the **Share** button (a square with an arrow pointing up) and tap it.

3. **Choose a Sharing Option**:

    - Select **Messages** to send the photo via text.

    - Tap **Mail** to attach the photo to an email.

    - Choose **AirDrop** to instantly share it with nearby Apple devices.

Sharing Multiple Photos at Once

- From the **Photos** app, tap **Select** in the top-right corner.

- Tap on each photo you want to share (a checkmark will appear).

- Tap the **Share** button and choose your preferred method of sharing.

Creating Shared Albums

Shared Albums let you collaborate with loved ones by allowing everyone to add photos and comments.

- Open the Photos app and navigate to Albums. Tap the plus (+) button.

- Select "New Shared Album" and give it a name, such as "Family Vacation."

- Invite others by entering their Apple ID email addresses.

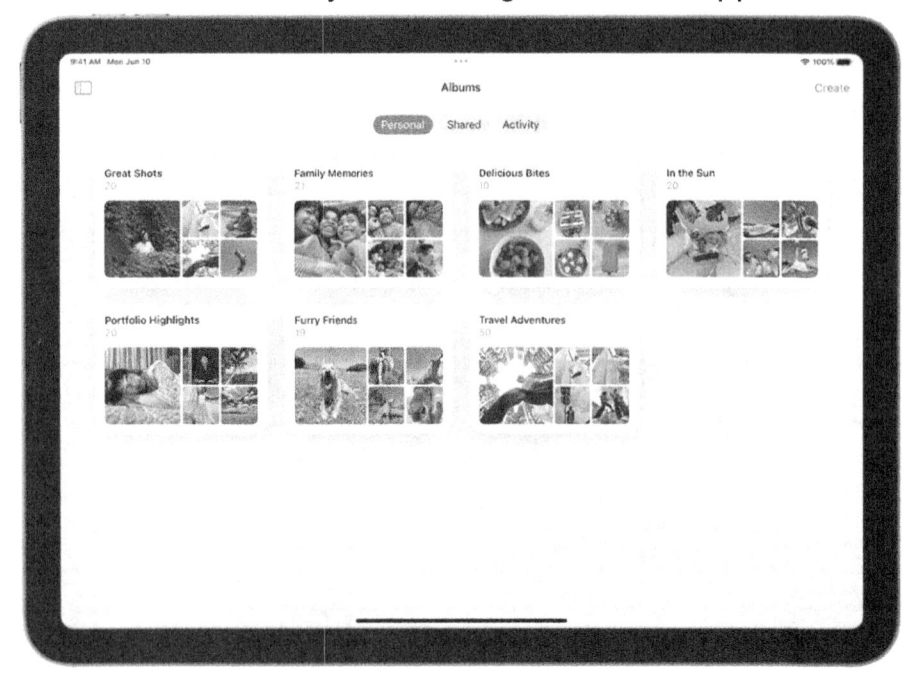

Using Files to Share Documents and More

The Files app on your iPad serves as a virtual filing cabinet, making it easy to organize and share documents, PDFs, and various other file types.

Finding Your Files

- Open the **Files** app on your iPad.

- Navigate through locations like **iCloud Drive, On My iPad,** or connected cloud services such as Google Drive or Dropbox.

Sharing Files

1. Locate the file you want to share and tap on it.

2. Tap the **Share** button.

3. Choose your sharing method:

    - **AirDrop** for nearby Apple devices.

    - **Mail** to send the file as an email attachment.

    - **Messages** to send directly to a contact.

Using iCloud Links for Larger Files

For files too large to send via email, use iCloud links:

- Tap the **Share** button and choose **Copy iCloud Link**.

- Paste the link into a text message or email for the recipient to download the file.

AirDrop: Instant Sharing Made Simple

AirDrop is one of the easiest ways to share photos, videos, and files with other Apple devices.

Enabling AirDrop

1. Open the **Control Center** by swiping down from the top-right corner of the screen.

2. Press and hold the box with the Wi-Fi and Bluetooth icons.

3. Tap **AirDrop** and choose **Contacts Only** or **Everyone** (the latter is useful for quick sharing).

Using AirDrop to Share

1. Select the photo, file, or document you want to share and tap the **Share** button.

2. Choose the recipient's device from the list of nearby **AirDrop** users.

3. The recipient will see a pop-up notification to accept the file.

Tips for Hassle-Free Sharing

1. **Organize Before Sharing**:

   - Use albums in Photos or folders in Files to keep everything tidy and easy to locate.

2. **Check Your Connection**:

   - Ensure your iPad is connected to Wi-Fi or has Bluetooth enabled for methods like AirDrop.

3. **Protect Your Privacy**:

   - Be cautious when sharing files containing sensitive information. Verify the recipient before sending.

4. **Monitor Storage**:

   - Large files can take up significant storage. Delete unnecessary duplicates after sharing.

Sharing photos and files is more than just a practical task—it's a way to strengthen relationships and keep the important moments of life flowing between you and your loved ones. Your iPad makes it simple, secure, and efficient, allowing you to focus on what matters most: staying connected.

Boosting Your Productivity

Setting Up and Using the Calendar App

Your iPad's **Calendar** app is a powerful tool that helps you stay organized, remember important dates, and manage your time efficiently. Whether you're scheduling doctor's appointments, family gatherings, or daily reminders, the Calendar app ensures you never miss a beat. In this sub-chapter, we'll guide you through setting up the app, adding events, and using its features to streamline your schedule.

Getting Started with the Calendar App

Opening the Calendar App

The Calendar app comes pre-installed on your iPad. To open it:

1. Locate the **Calendar** icon on your Home Screen—it resembles a white square with a red header displaying today's date.

2. Tap the icon to launch the app.

When you first open the Calendar app, it may prompt you to sign in with your Apple ID if you haven't done so already. This ensures your calendar can sync across all your Apple devices.

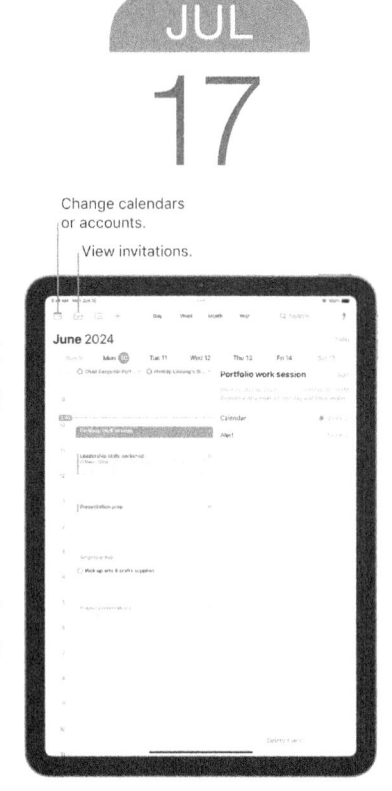

Syncing Your Calendar

You can link the Calendar app to other accounts, such as Google, Microsoft Outlook, or Yahoo, to consolidate all your schedules in one place.

1. Open the **Settings** app.

2. Scroll down and tap **Calendar**.

3. Select **Accounts > Add Account**.

4. Choose your account type, enter your login details, and toggle **Calendar** on to enable syncing.

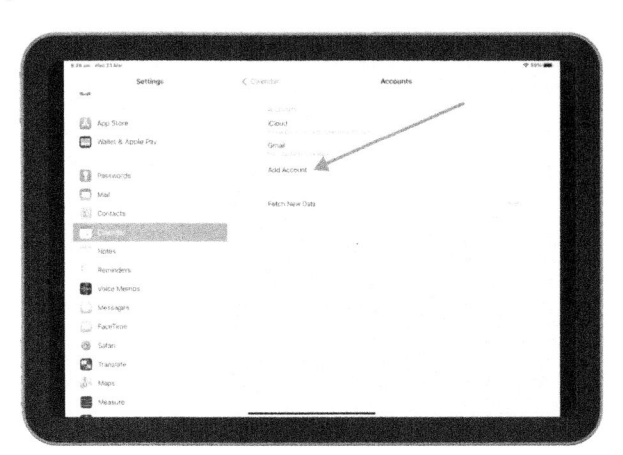

Adding and Managing Events

Creating a New Event

Adding an event is simple and helps you keep track of appointments, birthdays, or tasks.

1. Open the **Calendar app** and tap the **+** icon in the top-right corner.

2. Fill in the event details:

    - **Title**: Name your event (e.g., "Dentist Appointment").

    - **Location**: Add an address or place.

    - **Time**: Set the start and end times.

    - **Repeat**: Choose if the event should repeat daily, weekly, or yearly.

3. Tap **Add** to save the event.

Setting Alerts and Notifications

Stay on top of your schedule by enabling alerts.

1. When you are creating or editing an event, be sure to scroll down to the **Alert section**.

2. Choose when you'd like to be notified (e.g., 10 minutes before, 1 day before).

3. You'll receive a notification at the specified time, ensuring you're always prepared.

Editing or Deleting Events

- To edit, tap the event and then tap **Edit** in the top-right corner. Make your changes and tap **Done**.

- To delete it, open the event, scroll down, and tap **Delete Event**.

Exploring Calendar Views

The Calendar app offers multiple views to suit your planning style:

1. **Day View**: See a detailed timeline of your day's events.

2. **Week View**: Get a snapshot of your weekly schedule.

3. **Month View**: View all events in a month at a glance—perfect for long-term planning.

4. **Year View**: Navigate through the entire year to quickly locate specific dates.

To switch views, tap the corresponding icon at the top of the screen or pinch the screen to zoom in or out.

Using Shared Calendars

Shared calendars are a fantastic way to coordinate schedules with family members or groups.

1. In the Calendar app, tap **Calendars** at the bottom of the screen.

2. Tap the **i** icon next to the calendar you want to share.

3. Select **Add Person** and enter their email address.

4. Once they accept the invitation, both of you can view and edit the shared calendar.

Shared calendars are great for managing family events, group projects, or travel plans.

Tips for Maximizing the Calendar App

1. **Color-Code Your Events**:
   - Assign different colors to calendars (e.g., red for personal, blue for work) to easily distinguish between activities.
   - Tap **Calendars > Add Calendar**, then choose a color for your new calendar.

2. **Use Siri for Quick Scheduling**:
   - Say, **"Hey Siri, add a meeting to my calendar for tomorrow at 3 PM,"** and Siri will handle the rest.

3. **Link Events to Apps**:
   - If you receive an email with an event invitation, tap Add to Calendar to import it directly.

4. **Enable Time Zone Support**:
   - In **Settings > Calendar > Time Zone Support**, enable this feature to manage events across different time zones—useful for travel.

The Calendar app transforms your iPad into a personal assistant, helping you stay organized and manage your time with ease. With its user-friendly interface, coupled with powerful features, you'll never miss an important date again.

Writing Notes and Making Lists with the Notes App

The **Notes** app on your iPad is a versatile tool that makes organizing thoughts, creating to-do lists, and storing important information effortless. Whether you're jotting down a quick idea, keeping a shopping list, or drafting longer notes, this app is your digital notepad. In this sub-chapter, we'll explore how to use the Notes app effectively to enhance your productivity.

Getting Started with the Notes App

Launching the Notes App

The Notes app is pre-installed on your iPad, and you can access it by tapping its yellow and white icon on the Home Screen. If you've signed in with your Apple ID, Notes syncs seamlessly across all your Apple devices, ensuring you always have access to your content.

Creating Your First Note

1. Open the **Notes** app.

2. Tap the **New Note** icon (a square with a pencil) in the top-right corner.

3. Start typing your note using the on-screen keyboard.

4. To save, simply exit the note by tapping **Notes** in the top-left corner. Your note will be automatically stored in the app.

Writing Notes: From Text to Rich Content

Adding Rich Text and Formatting

The Notes app lets you add more than just plain text, turning your notes into visually appealing and organized documents.

1. Tap the **Aa** icon above the keyboard to access formatting options.

2. Choose from headings, bold, italic, or underline styles to emphasize key points.

3. Use bullet points, checklists, or numbered lists to structure your content.

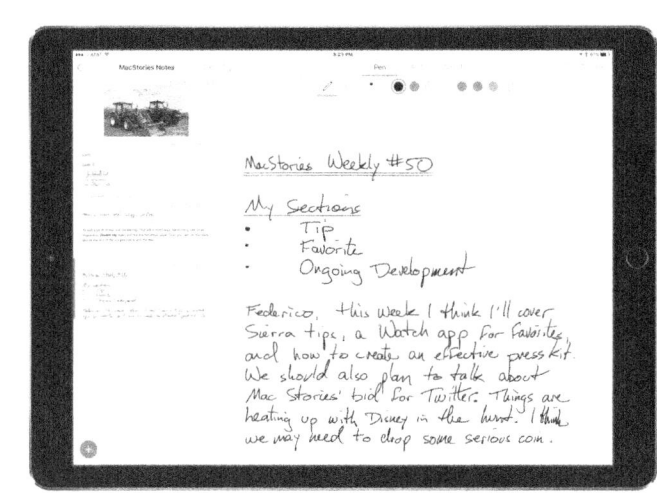

Inserting Images and Links

Add context or visual aids to your notes:

- To insert a photo or scan a document, tap the **Camera** icon and follow the prompts.

- To add a link, paste the URL directly into the note, and it will appear as a clickable link.

Drawing and Handwriting

For those who prefer a more hands-on approach:

1. Tap the **Markup** icon (a pen tip) to access the drawing tools.

2. Use your finger or an Apple Pencil to draw sketches, write notes, or highlight text.

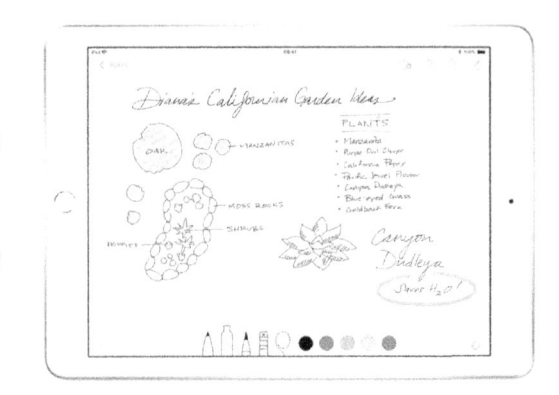

Making and Managing Lists

Creating Checklists

Checklists are perfect for grocery lists, packing lists, or task tracking.

1. Open a new or existing note.

2. Tap the **Checklist** icon (a circle with a checkmark) above the keyboard.

3. Type your first item, press Return, and continue adding items.

As you complete tasks, tap the circle next to an item to check it off.

Organizing Your Notes with Folders

To keep your notes and lists easily accessible, organize them into folders:

1. Tap the **Folders** button in the top-left corner.

2. Tap **New Folder** at the bottom.

3. Name your folder and tap **Save**.

4. Drag and drop notes into folders for better organization.

Pinning Important Notes

Keep your most-used lists or notes at the top for quick access:

1. Swipe right on a note in the list view.
2. Tap the **Pin** icon.
   Pinned notes appear at the top of your list, separated from other notes.

Advanced Features for Power Users

Sharing Notes with Others

Collaborate with family or friends by sharing notes:

1. Open the note you want to share.
2. Tap the **Share** icon (a square with an arrow).
3. Select a sharing method (e.g., Messages, Mail, or AirDrop).

You can also enable **collaboration** to allow others to edit the note in real time.

Using Tags for Quick Search

Tags help you categorize notes for easier retrieval:

1. In a note, type #tagname (e.g., #recipes) anywhere.
2. Tags are automatically indexed, and you can search for them by tapping the Tags browser.

Syncing Notes Across Devices

To access your notes on all Apple devices, ensure **iCloud Sync** is enabled:

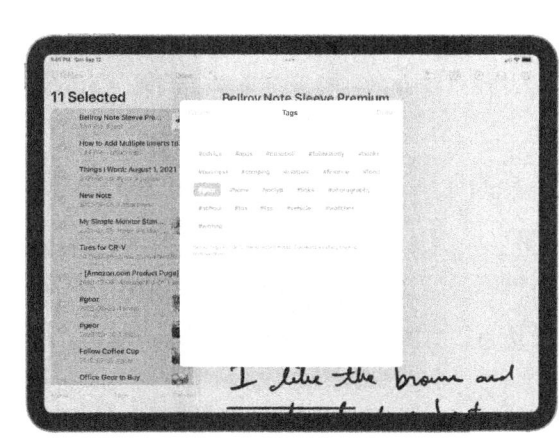

1. Go to **Settings > [Your Name] > iCloud**.
2. Toggle Notes to **On**.

Tips for Effective Note-Taking

1. **Use Siri for Hands-Free Notes**: Say, "Hey Siri, create a new note," and dictate your thoughts.
2. **Utilize Templates**: For recurring types of notes, create templates for quicker input.
3. **Search for Notes**: Use the search bar at the top of the Notes app to find notes by keywords, tags, or content.

The Notes app is more than just a digital notepad—it's a productivity powerhouse that helps you keep your life organized. With features that range from simple text input to advanced collaboration tools, it's an essential companion for managing tasks, jotting ideas, and staying on top of your responsibilities.

Stop Forgetting with the Use of Reminders

Staying organized and on top of tasks can be a challenge for anyone, but with your iPad, it's easier than ever to make sure you never forget an important appointment, task, or to-do. In this sub-chapter, we'll explore how to use the **Reminders** app on your iPad to stay organized and reduce the risk of forgetting important tasks.

What Is the Reminders App?

The **Reminders** app is a built-in tool on your iPad that helps you create, manage, and organize reminders for personal or professional tasks. Whether it's a doctor's appointment, picking up groceries, or a simple note to call a friend, Reminders can help you stay on track. The app allows you to set notifications, categorize reminders, and even share tasks with others, making it one of the most useful productivity tools on your device.

Getting Started with Reminders

To open the **Reminders** app on your iPad, simply tap the **Reminders** icon on your Home Screen. Once inside, you'll notice a simple and user-friendly interface that allows you to manage all of your tasks in one place.

Here's how you can start using it:

1. **Create a New Reminder**:
   - Tap the **Add List** button to create a new list if you want to categorize your reminders, such as "Shopping," "Work," or "Health."
   - To create a reminder, tap the New Reminder button and type the task you need to remember.
   - For example, if you need to pick up milk, type "Pick up milk" in the reminder field.

2. **Add Details to Your Reminder**:
   - After typing the task, you can tap on the i (information) button next to the reminder to add more details.
   - You can set a specific time for the reminder, choose to repeat the task, or even add a location-based reminder (for instance, a reminder to pick up milk when you're near the grocery store).

Setting Time-Based Reminders

One of the standout features of Reminders is the ability to set time-based alerts. This is perfect for appointments, deadlines, and any task that needs to be completed at a certain time. **Here's how to do it**:

1. After creating your reminder, tap on the **i** icon next to it.
2. Under **Date & Time**, turn on the toggle for **Remind me on a day**.
3. Set the date and time for when you want to be reminded.
4. Tap **Add** to save the reminder.

The app will now alert you at the set time, ensuring that you don't forget. You can also choose whether to be reminded **at a specific time**, **when leaving or arriving at a location**, or **at a set interval**.

Location-Based Reminders

Another valuable feature is the **location-based reminder**. This allows you to set reminders that are triggered based on your physical location. For instance, you could set a reminder to call a friend when you leave your home or pick up your prescriptions when you're near the pharmacy.

Here's how to set it up:

1. Tap the **i** icon next to your reminder.
2. Turn on **Remind me at a location**.
3. Choose your location by searching for an address or using your current location.
4. Tap **Add** to set the location.

The next time you arrive at or leave the specified location, your iPad will send you a notification reminding you of the task.

Organizing Reminders with Lists and Tags

To keep your reminders organized and easier to manage, you can group them into lists. For example, create separate lists for tasks related to **Home, Work, or Shopping**.

1. **Creating a List**: Tap **Add List** at the bottom left of the Reminders screen. Then, name your list (e.g., "Shopping List," "Medical Appointments," etc.).

2. **Adding to Lists**: When creating or editing a reminder, select which list it should belong to. You can even drag reminders between lists if you need to reorganize them.

3. **Using Tags**: You can tag reminders for quick searches. Tags might include keywords such as "urgent," "important," or "today." This helps you quickly filter your reminders and prioritize tasks based on your needs.

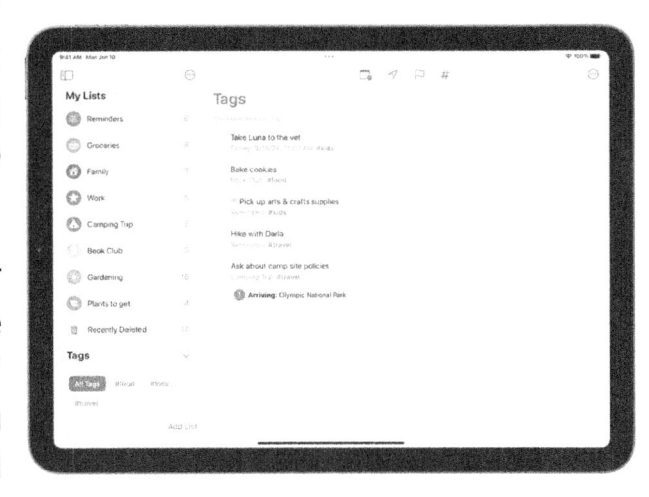

Collaborating on Reminders

If you're working on a task or project with someone, you can easily share reminders with others. This feature is perfect for household chores, joint appointments, or group tasks. To share a reminder list:

1. Tap the **three dots** in the upper-right corner of a list.

2. Select **Share List** and choose who you want to share it with. You can send an invitation via email or message.

3. Anyone with the shared list can add or mark reminders as complete, making collaboration easy.

Marking Tasks as Complete

Once you've completed a task, you can check it off the list to mark it as done. This not only gives you a sense of accomplishment but also helps keep you on track. To check off a task:

- Simply tap the circle next to the reminder to mark it as completed. The task will be crossed out, and you can focus on the remaining items.

Reminders for All Your Needs

Whether you're trying to keep track of important events, set up daily routines, or simply remind yourself to check off items on a shopping list, the **Reminders** app on your iPad is an invaluable tool. It's more than just a to-do list; it's a comprehensive assistant that helps you stay organized, manage time efficiently, and eliminate the chance of forgetting key tasks.

By setting up alerts, organizing your tasks by lists, and collaborating with others, you can streamline your daily routine and boost your productivity with minimal effort.

Voice Assistance with Siri: Your Virtual Helper

Imagine having a personal assistant ready to help at a moment's notice—one that never forgets, operates hands-free, and can perform tasks quickly and efficiently. Siri, Apple's voice assistant, brings this convenience to your fingertips (or voice). Whether you need a quick answer, a scheduled reminder, or help sending a message, Siri is your go-to virtual helper on the iPad.

In this sub-chapter, we'll explore how to activate Siri, use its voice commands, and unlock its potential to simplify your daily life.

Activating Siri: Getting Started

Siri can be accessed in multiple ways, depending on your preference and settings. Here's how to get started:

Option 1: Voice Activation with "Hey Siri"

1. Go to **Settings > Siri & Search**.
2. Toggle on **Listen for 'Hey Siri.'**

3. Follow the on-screen instructions to train Siri to recognize your voice.
   Once activated, simply say, "Hey Siri," followed by your command (e.g., "Hey Siri, what's the weather today?").

Option 2: Using the Home or Top Button

For iPads with a Home button, press and hold it to activate Siri.
For newer models without a Home button, press and hold the **Top Button**. Release the button once you see the Siri interface.

Option 3: Typing to Siri

If you prefer typing instead of speaking:

1. Go to **Settings > Accessibility > Siri**.

2. Enable **Type to Siri**.
   Now, when you activate Siri, a text input field appears instead of the voice interface.

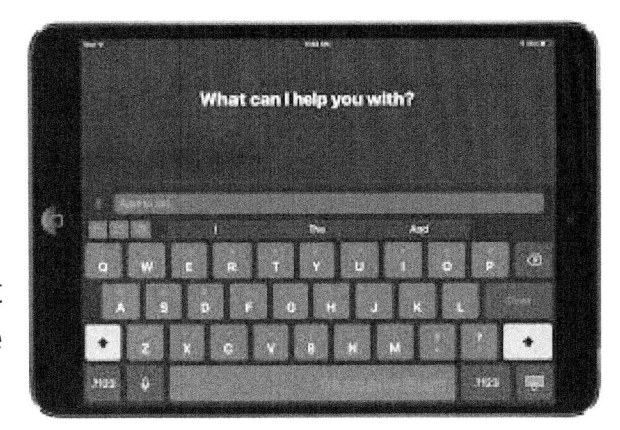

Using Siri for Everyday Tasks

Asking Questions

Siri is equipped to answer a variety of questions, from basic queries to complex searches. Try asking:

- "What's the current time in Tokyo?"
- "What are the top headlines today?"
- "How do you spell 'accommodate'?"

Sending Messages and Making Calls

With Siri, staying connected is effortless:

- **To send a message**: "Hey Siri, send a message to Mary saying, 'I'll be there at 5 PM.'"

- **To make a FaceTime call**: "Hey Siri, FaceTime John."

Setting Reminders and Alarms

Siri excels at helping you stay organized:

- "Hey Siri, remind me to feed the dogs at 3 PM."
- "Set an alarm for 7 AM tomorrow."

Managing Your Schedule

Siri integrates seamlessly with your calendar and helps you keep track of appointments:

- "Hey Siri, add a dentist appointment to my calendar for next Tuesday at 10 AM."
- "What's on my schedule for today?"

Boosting Productivity with Advanced Siri Features

Controlling Apps and Features

Siri can interact with many of your iPad's apps:

- **Emails**: "Hey Siri, check if I have any new emails."
- **Music**: "Play some relaxing music."
- **Maps**: "Give me directions to the nearest grocery store."

Using Siri Shortcuts

Siri Shortcuts automate routine tasks for efficiency:

1. Open the **Shortcuts** app.
2. Browse or create custom shortcuts (e.g., sending a daily weather update).
3. Invoke these shortcuts by saying their assigned phrase, like "Hey Siri, morning routine."

Dictation and Notes

Use Siri to dictate text for hands-free input:

- "Hey Siri, take a note: Remember to call Susan tomorrow."

- While in a text field, tap the **Microphone** icon and start speaking. Siri will convert your speech into text.

Customizing Siri to Suit Your Needs

Change Siri's Voice and Language

Make Siri feel more personal by customizing its voice:

1. Go to **Settings > Siri & Search > Siri Voice**.

2. Choose from a variety of accents and genders.

If you speak multiple languages, you can change Siri's language under **Settings > Siri & Search > Language.**

Adjusting Siri's Responses

For privacy or reduced interruptions, modify how Siri responds:

1. Navigate to **Settings > Siri & Search > Siri Responses.**
2. Choose whether Siri speaks, shows text, or stays silent based on your preferences.

Enabling Siri Suggestions

Siri can learn your habits and suggest useful actions:

- Enable **Siri Suggestions** under **Settings > Siri & Search** to get proactive prompts, such as contacting frequent callers or opening apps you use often.

Practical Tips for Using Siri Effectively

1. **Be Clear and Specific**: Siri works best with clear instructions. Instead of saying, "Remind me later," specify, "Remind me at 4 PM to call Tom."

2. **Explore Siri's Potential**: Experiment with different commands. Siri can perform a surprising range of tasks, from flipping a coin to translating phrases.

3. **Combine Siri with Accessibility Features**: If you have vision or mobility challenges, Siri integrates with features like VoiceOver and AssistiveTouch for enhanced accessibility.

Siri is a powerful, time-saving tool that enhances your iPad experience to make it more efficient and enjoyable.. From answering questions to automating tasks, Siri is your reliable virtual assistant, ready to help whenever you need it.

Entertainment at Your Fingertips

Streaming Movies and Shows with Netflix, Hulu, and More

Your iPad is a portable entertainment powerhouse, capable of bringing the latest movies, TV shows, and documentaries right to your fingertips. Streaming platforms like Netflix, Hulu, and others offer endless entertainment options, all accessible from the comfort of your home or on the go. In this sub-chapter, we'll guide you through setting up these services, exploring their features, and enjoying your favorite content effortlessly.

Step 1: Downloading and Setting Up Streaming Apps

To start streaming, you'll need to install the appropriate app for your chosen service. Here's how:

1. **Open the App Store**:
   - Tap the blue App Store icon on your home screen.

2. **Search for Your App**:
   - Tap the search bar at the top and type the name of the streaming service, such as "Netflix" or "Hulu."

3. **Download the App**:
   - Tap the app's name in the search results, then tap Get or the cloud icon. Authenticate with your Apple ID if prompted.

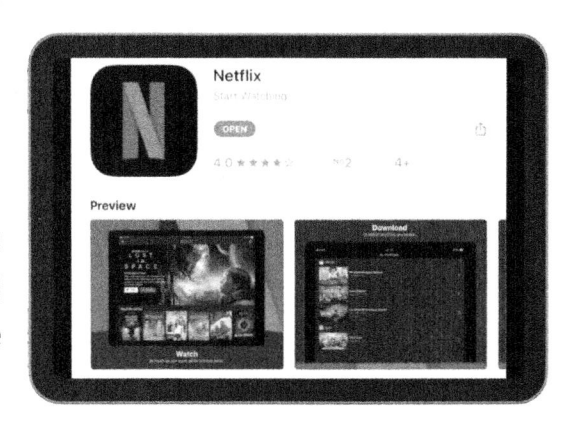

4. **Open and Sign In**:

    o Once the download is complete, tap Open. Enter your account credentials (email and password).

Tip: If you don't have an account yet, most apps offer an option to sign up directly within the app or on their website.

Step 2: Browsing and Discovering Content

Streaming services are designed to be intuitive, offering a wide range of genres, categories, and personalized recommendations. Here's how to explore:

Netflix

- **Home Screen**: Netflix displays personalized suggestions based on your viewing history.
- **Categories**: Scroll through categories like Action, Drama, or Comedy. Tap Search (magnifying glass icon) to look for specific titles or actors.
- **Profiles**: Create separate profiles for yourself and family members to keep recommendations tailored.

Hulu

- **Featured Content**: Hulu often showcases trending shows and new releases on the main screen.
- **Hubs**: Navigate through "Hubs" like TV Shows, Movies, or Networks to find content by type or provider.
- **My Stuff**: Add shows or movies to your personal library for quick access later.

Other Apps

- **Disney+**: This is Great for family-friendly options, including Disney classics and Marvel movies.

- **Amazon Prime Video**: A vast library of movies and TV shows, including exclusive originals.

- **Apple TV+**: Apple's own streaming service, featuring high-quality original content.

Step 3: Watching Content

Once you've found something to watch, start enjoying your selection:

1. **Tap to Play**: Tap the show or movie you want, then press the Play button.

2. **Use Playback Controls**:

   - Pause, rewind, or fast-forward using the on-screen controls.

   - Tap the Subtitles icon to enable captions or change languages if available.

3. **Adjust Video Quality**:

   - Apps usually adjust quality automatically based on your internet speed. For a manual option, check the app settings under Playback Quality.

Tip: If you experience buffering, ensure you're connected to a stable Wi-Fi network.

Step 4: Downloading for Offline Viewing

Heading on a trip or have limited internet access? Many apps allow you to download shows and movies to watch offline.

1. **Look for the Download Icon**:

   - On Netflix or Hulu, it's often a downward arrow next to eligible content.

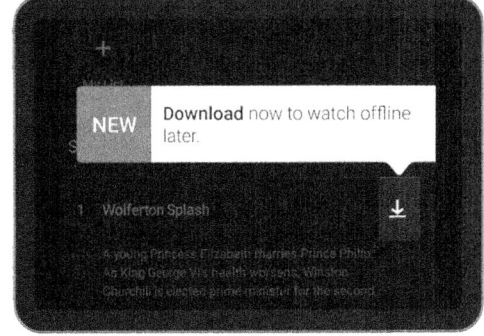

2. **Tap to Download**:

    o Select the download icon and wait for the process to complete.

3. **Access Offline Content**:

    o Go to the Downloads section in the app to find your saved titles.

Note: Downloads may expire after a certain period or become unavailable if the content is removed from the platform.

Step 5: Creating Watchlists

A watchlist helps you keep track of shows and movies you want to watch later.

- **Add to Watchlist**: Look for the "**Add to My List**" or "**Add to Watchlist**" button.

- **Organize Your List**: Some apps let you reorder or categorize items in your watchlist.

- **Access Anytime**: Your watchlist is easily accessible from the app's main menu.

Tips for an Enhanced Streaming Experience

1. Optimize Audio and Visual Settings

- Use Bluetooth headphones or external speakers for better sound quality.

- Adjust your screen's brightness in Control Center for optimal viewing.

2. Parental Controls

- If grandchildren use your iPad, enable parental controls to restrict age-inappropriate content.

- In Netflix, go to **Account Settings > Parental Controls** to set a PIN or restrict profiles.

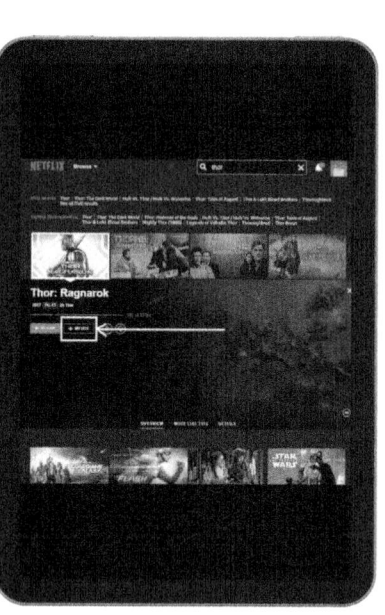

3. Use a Larger Screen

- Stream your content to a TV using **AirPlay** or an HDMI adapter for a cinematic experience.
- Open **Control Center**, tap **Screen Mirroring**, and select your Apple TV or compatible device.

Common Issues and Solutions

- **Can't Log In**: Double-check your email and password. Reset them through the app or website if needed.
- **Buffering Problems**: Ensure a stable Wi-Fi connection and close other apps using bandwidth.
- **App Crashes**: Update the app via the App Store or restart your iPad.

Streaming services like Netflix, Hulu, and others open the door to a world of entertainment. Whether you enjoy binge-watching series, discovering new movies, or reliving classics, your iPad makes it all simple and accessible. By learning to navigate these apps and customize your experience, you'll ensure countless hours of enjoyment, tailored to your tastes.

Listening to Music and Podcasts

The iPad is your personal gateway to a world of music and podcasts. Whether you're looking to revisit timeless classics, discover new hits, or dive into captivating podcast stories, your iPad offers an array of apps and features to enrich your listening experience. In this sub-chapter, you'll learn how to explore music streaming services, manage playlists, and enjoy podcasts like a pro.

Step 1: Setting Up Music Streaming Apps

Music streaming services provide access to millions of songs at your fingertips. Here's how to get started with popular apps like **Apple Music, Spotify,** and others.

Apple Music

1. **Open the Music App**: Pre-installed on your iPad, this app serves as a hub for streaming, downloading, and organizing your music.

2. **Sign Up or Sign In**: If you're new to Apple Music, tap Try It Free to explore a free trial. If you already have an account, sign in with your Apple ID.

3. **Browse and Play**: Explore curated playlists, albums, or genres by tapping the Search icon. To play a song, simply tap its title.

Spotify

1. **Download Spotify**: Open the App Store, search for "Spotify," and download it.

2. **Create an Account**: Sign up for free or upgrade to Spotify Premium for ad-free listening and offline downloads.

3. **Explore Playlists**: Spotify offers pre-made playlists like "Chill Hits" or "Top 50 Global," making it easy to find music for any mood.

Tip: You can use other apps like Pandora, Amazon Music, or YouTube Music if they better suit your needs.

Step 2: Creating and Managing Playlists

Playlists help you organize songs for specific moods, occasions, or themes. Here's how to make one:

1. **Start a Playlist:** In Apple Music, tap **Library > Playlists > New Playlist**. In Spotify, tap **Your Library > Create Playlist**.

2. **Add Songs:** Search for a song, then tap the **Add** or **+** icon to include it in your playlist.

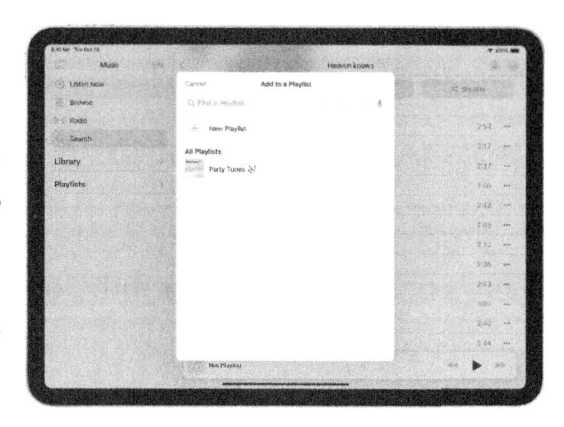

3. **Customize It:** Name your playlist, add a description, and rearrange the order of songs by dragging and dropping them.

4. **Play and Share:** Tap your playlist to start listening. Share it with friends by selecting the Share option and choosing a platform like Messages or Email.

Step 3: Discovering Podcasts

Podcasts are a fantastic way to learn, laugh, and stay entertained. From storytelling and interviews to educational series, there's a podcast for everyone.

Apple Podcasts

1. **Open the Podcasts App**: Another pre-installed app on your iPad, ready to explore.

2. **Search and Subscribe**: Tap the Search icon, type a topic or show name, and hit Subscribe to receive updates for new episodes.

3. **Download Episodes**: Tap the download icon next to an episode for offline listening.

Spotify and Third-Party Apps

Spotify also offers a rich podcast library, accessible under the **Podcasts & Shows** tab. You can also try apps like **Overcast, Pocket Casts,** or **Google Podcasts** for specialized features.

Tip: Many podcasts are free, but some apps offer premium subscriptions for ad-free or exclusive content.

Step 4: Enhancing Your Listening Experience

Your iPad offers several features to optimize music and podcast playback:

Using Headphones or Speakers

- **Bluetooth Headphones**: Connect your favorite wireless headphones in **Settings > Bluetooth** for a clutter-free experience.

- **External Speakers**: Pair your iPad with Bluetooth speakers for enhanced sound quality, perfect for a small gathering or a relaxing evening.

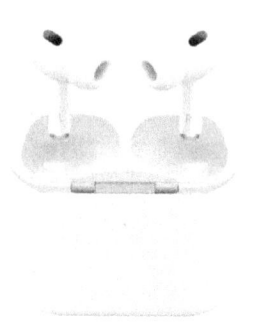

Customizing Playback Options

- Adjust the volume using the physical buttons or the Control Center slider.

- Skip backward or forward in podcasts by 15-30 seconds, depending on the app.

- Enable **Shuffle** or **Repeat** in the playback settings to mix up your music.

Offline Listening

- Save music and podcasts to your device for offline use by downloading them.

- Access these files in the **Downloads** or **Library** section of the respective app.

Tips for Enjoying Music and Podcasts to the Fullest

1. **Explore Curated Playlists**

    - Use playlists like "Daily Mix" (Spotify) or "For You" (Apple Music) for personalized recommendations.

2. **Set the Mood with Smart Playlists**

    - Create mood-based playlists for workouts, relaxation, or celebrations.

3. **Try Podcast Categories**

    - Browse categories such as comedy, health, technology, or true crime to find something intriguing.

4. **Sync Across Devices**
   - Enable iCloud for Apple Music or log in to Spotify across devices to access your library anywhere.

5. **Use Voice Commands**
   - Ask Siri to play a specific song, album, or podcast. For example, "Hey Siri, play my Relaxing playlist."

Troubleshooting Common Issues

- **Playback Stops Unexpectedly**: Ensure you have a stable internet connection or download content for uninterrupted listening.

- **Bluetooth Won't Connect**: Restart your iPad or reset your headphones and try pairing again.

- **Podcast Episodes Missing**: Check if the podcast requires a subscription or if episodes have been removed by the creator.

Listening to music and podcasts on your iPad offers endless enjoyment and discovery. With powerful apps and simple tools, you can create the perfect soundtrack for your day or dive into stories and conversations that captivate your imagination. In the next sub-chapter, we'll explore the world of eBooks and audiobooks, helping you turn your iPad into a portable library. Stay tuned!

Reading E-books and Magazines on the iPad

The iPad is your window to a vast library of books, magazines, and other reading materials—all available with just a few taps. Whether you love novels, enjoy informative magazines, or want to explore new interests, the iPad makes it easy to access and organize your favorite reads. In this sub-chapter, we'll guide you through the best apps, features, and techniques to get the most out of reading on your iPad.

Step 1: Exploring Apps for E-books and Magazines

There are several excellent apps for reading books and magazines on the iPad. Here's a breakdown of the most popular ones:

Apple Books

- **Pre-installed App**: Apple Books is the default app for reading e-books and audiobooks.

- **Browse the Store**: Open the app, tap **Book Store**, and explore categories like **Bestsellers** or **Free Books**.

- **Download Your First Book**: Tap a book title, select **Get** or **Buy**, and it will be added to your library.

Kindle by Amazon

- **Download the App**: Visit the App Store, search for "Kindle," and install it.

- **Sync Your Amazon Account**: Log in to access your purchased books.

- **Discover Kindle Unlimited**: If you subscribe, you can borrow thousands of books for a monthly fee.

Magazines via Apple News+

- **Apple News+ Subscription**: Subscribe to Apple News+ in the **News** app to access a wide range of magazines.

- **Browse Titles**: Find popular publications in categories like Travel, Food, or Entertainment.

- **Read Offline**: Download magazines to enjoy them even without an internet connection.

Step 2: Reading Features and Tools

Once you've selected your reading materials, familiarize yourself with these essential tools to enhance your reading experience:

Customizing Text Settings

- Open a book and tap the **Aa** icon.
- Adjust the font size, text style, and background color (e.g., light, dark, or sepia).
- Enable **Scrolling View** for continuous scrolling instead of page turns.

Highlighting and Taking Notes

- Tap and hold a word, then drag to select text.
- Choose **Highlight** or **Add Note** from the menu to mark important sections or jot down thoughts.
- Access all highlights and notes under the **Table of Contents** in Apple Books or the Kindle app.

Using the Dictionary and Search

- Tap and hold a word to view its definition or use the **Search** feature to find specific terms or topics within the book.

Audiobook Integration

- Switch between reading and listening by downloading the audiobook version of your e-book, if available.
- Use the **Playback Speed** feature to adjust narration to your preferred pace.

Step 3: Organizing and Managing Your Library

An organized library ensures you can easily find and enjoy your reading materials:

Creating Collections

- In Apple Books, tap **Library > Collections > New Collection**.

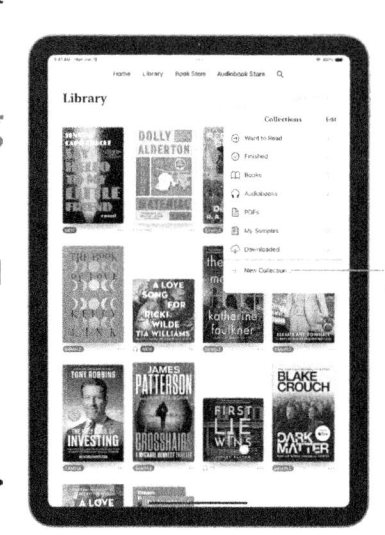

- Name the collection (e.g., "Mystery Novels" or "Cooking Guides") and add books to it.

- Similar features are available in the Kindle app under **Your Library**.

Syncing Across Devices

- Enable iCloud for Apple Books or log in to your Kindle/Amazon account to sync your reading progress, bookmarks, and notes across devices.

Deleting and Re-downloading Books

- Free up space by removing books you've finished. In Apple Books, tap the three-dot menu on a title and select **Remove**. You can re-download it anytime.

Step 4: Tips for an Enjoyable Reading Experience

Maximize your reading enjoyment with these tips:

1. **Adjust Screen Brightness**:
   - Use Control Center to dim your screen, reducing eye strain during nighttime reading.

2. **Try Dark Mode**:
   - Activate Dark Mode in the app settings or iPad's display settings for a comfortable reading experience in low light.

3. **Explore Free Content**:
   - Check out free e-books from your local library using apps like Libby or OverDrive.

4. **Set Reading Goals**:
   - Apple Books allows you to track reading time. Use this feature to stay motivated and build a regular reading habit.

5. **Offline Reading**:
    - Download books and magazines ahead of time to read on the go or in areas without internet access.

Troubleshooting Common Issues

- **Books Not Downloading**: Check your internet connection or verify sufficient storage space on your iPad.

- **App Crashes or Freezes:** Restart your iPad or update the app to the latest version.

- **Syncing Problems:** Ensure that iCloud or your Amazon account is properly set up and logged in.

With your iPad, the joy of reading is always within reach. From e-books to magazines, you can explore countless genres and topics tailored to your interests. Use the tools and tips outlined here to customize your experience, stay organized, and make the most of your iPad as a reading companion.

Exploring the World of Photos and Videos

Taking Stunning Photos with Your iPad Camera

Your iPad is more than just a device for browsing the internet or reading books—it's also equipped with a powerful camera, it is capable of capturing stunning images. Whether you want to document special moments, create artistic images, or share snapshots with loved ones, your iPad's camera is a versatile tool that's easy to use. In this sub-chapter, we'll explore how to take beautiful photos using your iPad and introduce you to the essential features that make photography a breeze.

Getting to Know the iPad Camera

Before diving into photography, it's important to familiarize yourself with the basic layout and functions of the iPad's Camera app:

Accessing the Camera App

1. **From the Home Screen**: Tap the Camera icon to open the app.
2. **Using Control Center**: Swipe down from the top-right corner and tap the camera icon.
3. **Lock Screen Shortcut**: Swipe left on the lock screen to instantly access the camera.

Understanding the Camera Interface

When you open the Camera app, you'll see several key elements:

- **Shutter Button**: The large white circle is for taking photos.
- **Zoom Control**: Pinch the screen to zoom in or out or use the zoom slider for precision.

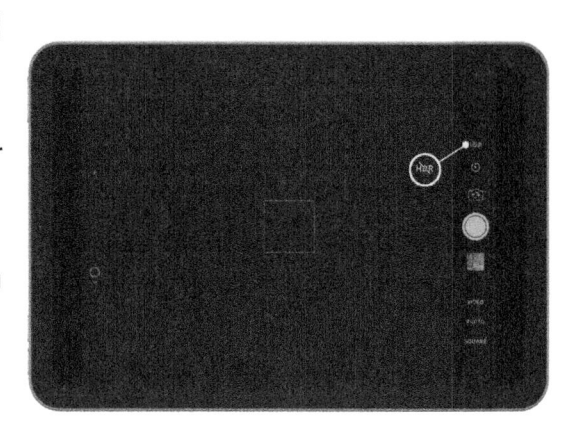

- **Switch Camera**: Tap the circular arrow icon to switch between the front and rear cameras.

- **Mode Selector**: Swipe through options like Photo, Portrait, and Panorama.

Taking Your First Photo

Follow these steps to ensure your photos look great:

Framing the Shot

1. Hold your iPad steady with both hands or use a stand for stability.

2. Position your subject within the frame. Use the **Rule of Thirds Grid** for balanced composition (enable this in **Settings > Camera > Grid**).

3. Ensure good lighting by facing the light source, such as a window or lamp, to avoid dark or blurry photos.

Focusing and Adjusting Exposure

- **Tap to Focus**: Tap on the subject in the frame to bring it into focus.

- **Adjust Exposure**: Once focused, swipe up or down on the screen to brighten or darken the image.

Using the Shutter Button or Volume Controls

- Tap the **Shutter Button** on the screen to capture the photo.

- Alternatively, press the **Volume Up** button on the side of your iPad for a more natural way to snap a picture.

Exploring Camera Features for Better Photos

Your iPad's Camera app includes features that can elevate your photography:

Portrait Mode (Available on Certain Models)

- Blur the background for professional-looking portraits.
- Select **Portrait** from the mode selector and follow the on-screen prompts for optimal results.

Live Photos

- Capture a few seconds of movement and sound before and after your photo.
- To enable Live Photos, tap the circular icon located at the top of the screen.

Panorama Mode

- Take wide, sweeping shots—perfect for landscapes or group photos.
- Select **Pano**, then move your iPad slowly across the scene while following the on-screen guide.

Timer

- Use the built-in timer for hands-free shots. Tap the clock icon and choose a 3 or 10-second delay.

Filters

- Experiment with built-in filters to enhance your photos. Tap the filter icon (three overlapping circles) and select options like Vivid or Noir.

Tips for Stunning Photos

Here are some expert tips to take your photography to the next level:

1. **Use Natural Light**: Outdoor lighting during early morning or late afternoon (golden hour) produces the most flattering photos.
2. **Avoid Zooming Too Much**: Excessive zooming can reduce image quality. Instead, move closer to your subject when possible.

3. **Experiment with Angles**: Experiment with photographing from various angles, such as low to the ground or overhead, to create more dynamic images.

4. **Keep the Lens Clean**: Carefully clean the camera lens using a microfiber cloth to prevent smudges and blurry photos.

5. **Use Burst Mode**: Press and hold the shutter button to take multiple photos in rapid succession, ensuring you capture the perfect moment.

Saving and Reviewing Your Photos

After taking photos, you can easily review and organize them:

Accessing Your Photos

- Open the **Photos** app to view all your images.
- Your latest photo will appear in the Recents album.

Deleting Unwanted Shots

- Select a photo, then tap the trash can icon to remove it. Don't worry—it's saved in the **Recently Deleted** folder for 30 days if you change your mind.

Sharing Photos

- Tap the **Share** icon (a square with an arrow) to send your photo via email, Messages, or social media.

Troubleshooting Common Issues

- **Blurry Photos**: Ensure the lens is clean and hold the iPad steady while taking the shot.
- **Low Light Challenges**: Enable the flash or use external lighting to brighten the scene.

- **Camera App Not Opening**: Restart your iPad or ensure it has enough storage space for new photos.

Taking stunning photos with your iPad is simple and enjoyable once you understand the basics and make use of the built-in features. With practice, you'll be able to capture memories, create artistic shots, and share your experiences with loved ones.

Editing Photos and Videos Like a Pro

One of the most exciting aspects of photography and videography on your iPad is the ability to not only capture stunning images and videos but also to edit them to perfection. Whether you want to enhance colors, crop out distractions, or add special effects, your iPad offers a wide array of editing tools that are both intuitive and powerful. In this sub-chapter, we'll walk you through the process of editing photos and videos, providing you with expert tips to help you create professional-looking results.

Editing Photos in the Photos App

Your iPad's **Photos** app is equipped with a robust set of editing tools that let you fine-tune every aspect of your photos. Here's how to get started:

Opening the Editing Tools

1. **Select a Photo**: Open the Photos app and tap on the image you want to edit.
2. **Enter Edit Mode**: Tap Edit in the top-right corner to access the editing tools.

Basic Adjustments

Once in edit mode, you'll see several icons along the bottom of the screen. Let's look at the most commonly used tools:

- **Auto-Enhance**: Tap the magic wand icon to automatically improve the photo's brightness, contrast, and color. This is a quick fix for most photos that need a little boost.

- **Filters:** Tap the filter icon (three overlapping circles) to apply a preset filter to your photo, such as **Vivid, Dramatic,** or **Mono**. This can drastically change the mood of your image with just one tap.

Fine-Tuning Your Image

For more detailed editing, use the following tools:

- **Exposure, Brilliance, and Highlights**: Slide the adjustment bar to lighten or darken your image, control how bright the highlights are, or adjust the overall brilliance of the photo.

- **Contrast and Brightness**: Increase or decrease the contrast to make the darks darker and the lights lighter. Brightness adjustments can bring out more details in shadows.

- **Saturation**: Use the saturation tool to make the colors more vivid or tone them down for a more muted look.

- **Sharpness**: Adjust the sharpness of your image to bring out more detail or smooth out graininess.

Cropping and Rotating

- **Crop**: Tap the crop icon to trim the edges of your photo, remove unwanted areas, or improve composition.

- **Rotate and Flip**: Tap the rotate icon to rotate your image in 90-degree increments or use the flip icon to mirror the photo horizontally.

- **Straightening**: If your photo is slightly tilted, use the straighten tool to fix the angle and make your horizon lines level.

Undoing Changes

If you ever make a mistake or want to return to the original photo, tap **Revert** to undo all changes and restore the image to its original form.

Editing Videos in the Photos App

Editing videos on your iPad is just as simple as editing photos. Here's how you can enhance your videos:

Trimming and Cutting

1. **Select a Video**: Open the Photos app and choose the video you want to edit.

2. **Enter Edit Mode**: Tap Edit in the top-right corner to start editing the video.

3. **Trim the Video**: Drag the sliders on either side of the video timeline to trim out unwanted sections at the beginning or end of the video. This is especially useful for cutting off excess footage or improving the pacing of your clip.

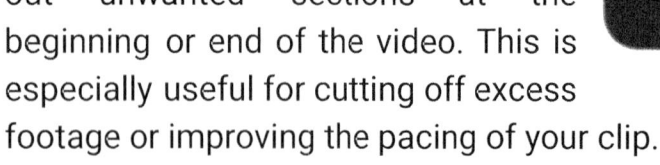

Adjusting Video Settings

Once the video is trimmed, you can adjust the following:

- **Exposure and Brightness**: Just like photos, videos can be enhanced by adjusting the exposure and brightness to make them clearer or more dramatic.

- **Filters**: Apply a filter to change the look and feel of the video. Tap the filter icon to apply a preset style like Vivid or Film Noir.

- **Volume Control**: Adjust the audio by sliding the volume control, whether to reduce background noise or enhance speech and music.

Cropping and Rotating the Video

You can also crop and rotate your video:

- **Crop**: Tap the crop icon to zoom in on the video or remove unwanted areas from the frame.

- **Rotate**: If you shot the video in the wrong orientation, tap the rotate button to fix it.

Adding Music and Effects

For added flair, you can add background music, sound effects, or voiceover:

- **Music**: Tap the **Music** icon to select a track from your music library or add a pre-recorded sound clip.

- **Voiceover**: Tap the **Voiceover** icon to record a voiceover directly into your video, which is ideal for explaining a moment or adding a personal touch.

Using Third-Party Apps for Advanced Editing

While the **Photos** app provides all the basic tools needed for editing, there are also third-party apps that offer more advanced editing features. Some popular options include:

Snapseed

Snapseed is a powerful app that offers a range of filters and editing tools to enhance photos and give them a professional touch. It includes features like **Selective Adjust**, which enables you to edit particular sections of a photo, and **Healing**, which lets you remove blemishes or distractions.

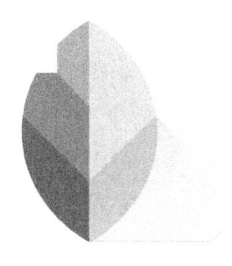

iMovie

For video editing, iMovie is an excellent option. It allows you to create movies with effects, transitions, and titles. You can also trim clips, adjust audio, and add music for a more polished video. iMovie is simple to use, but packed with powerful features for creating professional-looking videos.

Sharing and Saving Your Edited Photos and Videos

Once your photos and videos are edited to your liking, it's time to save and share them:

Saving Your Edits

- **Photos**: After editing, tap Done to save the changes to your photo. Your edited photo will overwrite the original, but don't worry—you can always revert to the original if needed.

- **Videos**: Tap Done after editing your video. The edited version will be saved in the Photos app.

Sharing Your Creations

- Share your edited photos and videos directly from the **Photos** app by tapping the **Share** icon. You can send them via **Email, Messages**, or upload them to **social media** platforms like Facebook and Instagram.

Troubleshooting Common Editing Issues

Here are a few common problems you might encounter while editing photos or videos, along with solutions:

- **Blurry Photos or Videos**: If your image or video becomes blurry after editing, try to adjust the sharpness or revert to the original version if the edits compromise the clarity.

- **Loss of Quality After Editing**: Avoid excessive filters or zooming in on photos, as this can reduce the quality of your image. Always save a copy of the original before making extensive edits.

- **App Crashes During Editing:** If an app crashes, try closing it and restarting your iPad. Ensure your iPad has sufficient storage space for the edits to be processed.

Editing photos and videos on your iPad is both accessible and enjoyable, offering tools that range from simple enhancements to professional-grade adjustments. With these editing skills, you can turn your everyday snapshots and videos into masterpieces, preserving your memories and sharing them with friends and family.

Creating Albums and Slideshows to Share Memories

Your iPad is more than just a tool for capturing photos and videos—it's a device that helps you organize and share cherished memories with ease. With features like albums and slideshows, you can curate your favorite moments into a cohesive collection and present them in a beautiful, dynamic format. This sub-chapter will guide you step-by-step through creating albums and slideshows that you can share with loved ones, ensuring your special memories are always at your fingertips.

Organizing Photos with Albums

Albums allow you to group related photos and videos together, making it easier to find and share specific memories. Whether it's a vacation, a family gathering, or a collection of favorite snapshots, creating an album is simple and intuitive.

Creating an Album

1. **Open the Photos App**: Tap on the Photos app from your iPad's home screen.

2. **Go to the Albums Tab**: At the bottom of the screen, tap the Albums tab to view all your current albums.

3. **Start a New Album**: Tap the + icon in the top-left corner, then select New Album.

4. **Name Your Album**: Type in a name for your album (e.g., "Hawaii Vacation 2024") and tap Save.

5. **Add Photos and Videos**: A list of your media will appear. Tap on the items you want to include in your album, then tap Done to finish. Your album is now ready and can be found in the Albums tab.

Managing Albums

- **Adding More Photos**: Open the album, tap the + icon, and select additional photos or videos to include.

- **Removing Photos**: To remove a photo from the album, tap Select, choose the image, and tap the trash icon. Don't worry—this won't delete the photo from your library; it only removes it from the album.

- **Rearranging Photos**: Tap and hold on a photo, then drag it to rearrange the order.

Creating Slideshows

Slideshows are an engaging way to relive memories, blending your photos and videos with music and transitions. They're perfect for sharing at family gatherings, sending to friends, or simply enjoying on your own.

Making a Slideshow in the Photos App

1. **Open an Album**: Start by opening the album containing the photos and videos you want to include in the slideshow.

2. **Select Slideshow**: Tap the More Options (three dots) icon in the top-right corner and choose Slideshow from the menu.

3. **Enjoy the Slideshow**: The Photos app will automatically generate a slideshow that includes transitions and background music.

Customizing Your Slideshow

For a more personalized slideshow, follow these steps:

1. **Pause the Slideshow**: Tap the screen while the slideshow is playing, then tap **Options** in the bottom-right corner.

2. **Choose Music**: Select **Music** to pick a song from your library or use one of Apple's preset tracks. Choose something that complements the mood of your photos.

3. **Change the Theme**: Under **Theme**, select from options like **Origami, Magazine**, or **Ken Burns** to alter the slideshow's visual style.

4. **Adjust the Speed**: Use the slider to make the slideshow play faster or slower.

5. **Replay and Share**: Tap **Done** to save your customizations. You can replay the slideshow anytime or share it with others via AirPlay, Messages, or email.

Sharing Albums and Slideshows

Once you've created an album or slideshow, sharing it with others is simple and rewarding.

Sharing an Album

1. **Select the Album**: Go to the Albums tab and tap the album you want to share.

2. **Tap the Share Icon**: In the top-right corner, tap the Share icon (a square with an arrow).

3. **Choose How to Share**: Select an option such as Messages, Mail, or AirDrop to share the album with your desired recipient.

Sharing a Slideshow

1. **Export as a Video**: Unfortunately, the Photos app doesn't directly allow you to save a slideshow as a video, but you can recreate it using third-party apps like **iMovie** or **Keynote**, where you can export it as a shareable file.

2. **Use AirPlay**: If you're sharing the slideshow in person, tap the **AirPlay** icon to display it on a nearby Apple TV or compatible device.

Using iCloud to Share Memories

iCloud makes it easy to share photos and albums with friends and family, especially if they also use Apple devices.

Creating a Shared Album

1. **Enable iCloud Photos**: Go to **Settings > [Your Name] > iCloud > Photos**, and turn on **iCloud Photos**.

2. **Create a Shared Album**: In the Photos app, tap **+** > **New Shared Album**. Name your album and invite others to join by entering their email addresses.

3. **Add Photos and Comments**: Include your favorite photos and videos. You and your invitees can add comments or contribute their own content.

Viewing Shared Memories

Shared albums allow everyone involved to view the collection at their leisure. They're a wonderful way to stay connected, especially with family members who live far away.

Troubleshooting and Tips

Here are some tips to ensure smooth album and slideshow creation:

- **Storage Concerns**: If you're running low on storage, consider using iCloud Photos to keep your albums and slideshows accessible without taking up local space.

- **Backing Up Memories**: Always back up your photos and albums using iCloud or an external hard drive to ensure your memories are safe.

- **Experiment with Styles:** Don't hesitate to explore different themes and music options for your slideshows. A small tweak can significantly enhance the presentation.

Creating albums and slideshows on your iPad transforms your digital photos into organized, shareable, and dynamic memories. Whether it's crafting a visual story of a family trip or compiling a heartfelt slideshow for a special occasion, these tools empower you to celebrate and share your moments with ease.

Staying Safe and Secure

Setting Up Passcodes, Face ID, and Touch ID

Your iPad is a powerful device that stores sensitive and personal information, such as photos, emails, contacts, and even financial details. Ensuring your device is secure is not only essential for protecting your data but also for your peace of mind. Apple provides several easy-to-use security features, including Passcodes, Face ID, and Touch ID, to help keep your iPad safe while maintaining convenient access. This sub-chapter will guide you step-by-step on how to set up these features and use them effectively.

Understanding iPad Security Features

Before diving into the setup, it's helpful to understand what each feature does:

- **Passcode**: A numeric or alphanumeric code you enter manually to unlock your device. It's the foundational security feature and is required to set up a Face ID or Touch ID.

- **Face ID**: Available on iPads with facial recognition hardware, this feature uses advanced technology to recognize your face and unlock your device instantly.

- **Touch ID**: Found on iPads with a Home button or top button sensor, Touch ID scans your fingerprint for secure and effortless access.

Each feature enhances your iPad's security while offering the convenience of quick access for trusted users.

Setting Up a Passcode

Your iPad requires a passcode during its initial setup, but if you skipped this step or want to change your passcode, follow these steps:

1. **Open Settings**: Open the Settings app located on your Home Screen

2. **Go to Passcode Options**: Scroll down and select Face ID & Passcode or Touch ID & Passcode (based on your iPad model).

3. **Enter Current Passcode**: If you already have a passcode, you'll need to enter it to access the settings.

4. **Set or Change Your Passcode**:

    - Tap **Turn Passcode On** if you don't have one yet, or **Change Passcode** to update an existing one.

    - Choose a passcode type: **6-digit numeric, 4-digit numeric, or Custom Alphanumeric.** Apple recommends the alphanumeric option for maximum security.

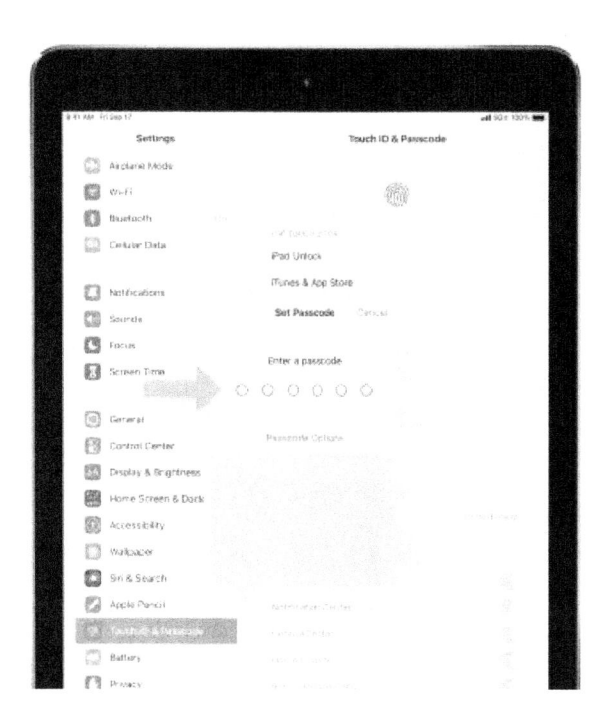

5. **Confirm Your Passcode**: Re-enter your chosen passcode to finalize the setup.

Pro Tip: Use a passcode that is easy for you to remember but difficult for others to guess. Avoid obvious choices like birthdays or "1234."

Setting Up Face ID

If your iPad supports Face ID, you can unlock your device with just a glance. It's fast, secure, and works even in low light.

1. **Access Face ID Settings**: Open Settings, then tap Face ID & Passcode.

2. **Enter Your Passcode**: Provide your passcode to proceed.

3. **Set Up Face ID**: Tap Set Up Face ID and follow the on-screen instructions:

    - Hold your iPad at eye level.

    - Position your face within the circular frame on the screen.

    - Slowly move your head in a circular motion to complete the scan.

4. **Complete the Process**: After two scans, Face ID will be set up. You can now unlock your iPad, authenticate purchases, and more by simply looking at your device.

Pro Tip: If you wear glasses or frequently change your appearance (e.g., with hats or makeup), Face ID can still recognize you. However, you can improve accuracy by enabling **Alternate Appearance** in the Face ID settings.

Setting Up Touch ID

For iPads equipped with a Touch ID sensor, fingerprint recognition provides another convenient way to secure your device.

1. **Open Touch ID Settings**: In Settings, tap Touch ID & Passcode.

2. **Enter Your Passcode**: Input your passcode to continue.

3. **Add a Fingerprint**: Tap Add a Fingerprint and follow these steps:
    - Place your finger on the sensor (either the Home button or the top button, depending on your iPad model).

- o Lift and rest your finger repeatedly as prompted.
- o Adjust your grip to ensure the sensor captures all parts of your fingerprint.

4. **Name Your Fingerprint**: To manage multiple fingerprints, you can label them (e.g., "Right Thumb," "Left Index Finger") for clarity.

Pro Tip: You can add up to five fingerprints, which is helpful if you want to use multiple fingers or allow trusted family members to access your iPad.

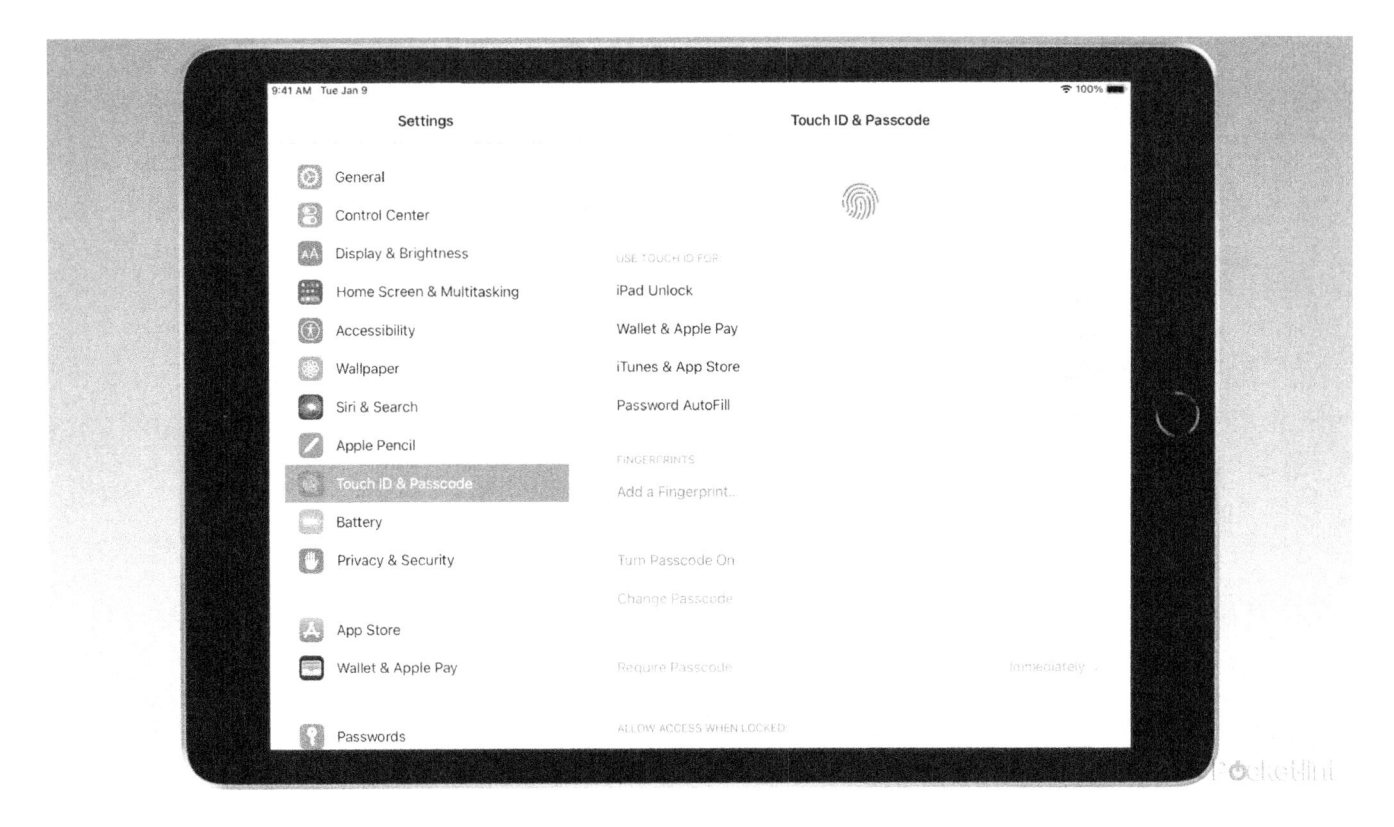

Enhancing Your Security

Once you've set up your preferred method of unlocking your iPad, take these additional steps to maximize security:

- **Enable Auto-Lock**: In **Settings > Display & Brightness**, set your iPad to lock automatically after a short period of inactivity. A 1- or 2-minute setting is ideal for balancing security and convenience.

- **Turn on Erase Data**: In the **Face ID & Passcode** or **Touch ID & Passcode settings**, toggle on **Erase Data**. This will erase all data on your iPad after 10 failed passcode attempts, protecting your information if your device is lost or stolen.

Troubleshooting Common Issues

- **Face ID Not Working**: Ensure your camera is clean and unobstructed. If issues persist, reset Face ID in the settings and scan your face again.

- **Touch ID Not Responding**: Wash and dry your hands, then try again. Re-registering your fingerprints can also resolve persistent issues.

- **Forgotten Passcode**: If you forget your passcode, you'll need to erase your iPad and restore it from a backup. Keep your Apple ID credentials handy for this process.

Setting up Passcodes, Face ID, and Touch ID on your iPad not only protects your personal information but also simplifies your access to the device. By following the steps outlined in this sub-chapter, you'll ensure that your iPad is both secure and easy to use. With your security features in place, you can confidently explore your iPad's capabilities, knowing your data is safe.

Recognizing and Avoiding Scams

The digital world offers countless benefits, from staying connected with loved ones to exploring new hobbies. However, it also comes with risks, such as online scams designed to trick unsuspecting users into sharing sensitive information or money. This sub-chapter will help you recognize common scams, take proactive steps to avoid them, and protect yourself while enjoying your iPad.

Understanding Common Scams

Scammers are always inventing new tricks, but many scams follow predictable patterns. Being familiar with these common schemes can help you identify and avoid them:

- **Phishing Emails and Messages**: These scams frequently appear as emails or text messages pretending to be from a trusted company, such as Apple, your bank, or a delivery service. They might ask you to click a link and provide personal information, such as your password or credit card details.

- **Tech Support Scams**: Scammers may claim your device is infected with a virus or malfunctioning, prompting you to call a fake support number. They might try to charge you for unnecessary services or steal your information.

- **Prize or Lottery Scams**: Emails or messages announcing you've won a prize or lottery (that you never entered) are a common ploy to trick you into paying fees or providing personal details.

- **Fake Websites and Apps**: Scammers can create fake websites or apps that look legitimate but are designed to steal your information. Always verify authenticity before entering sensitive information.

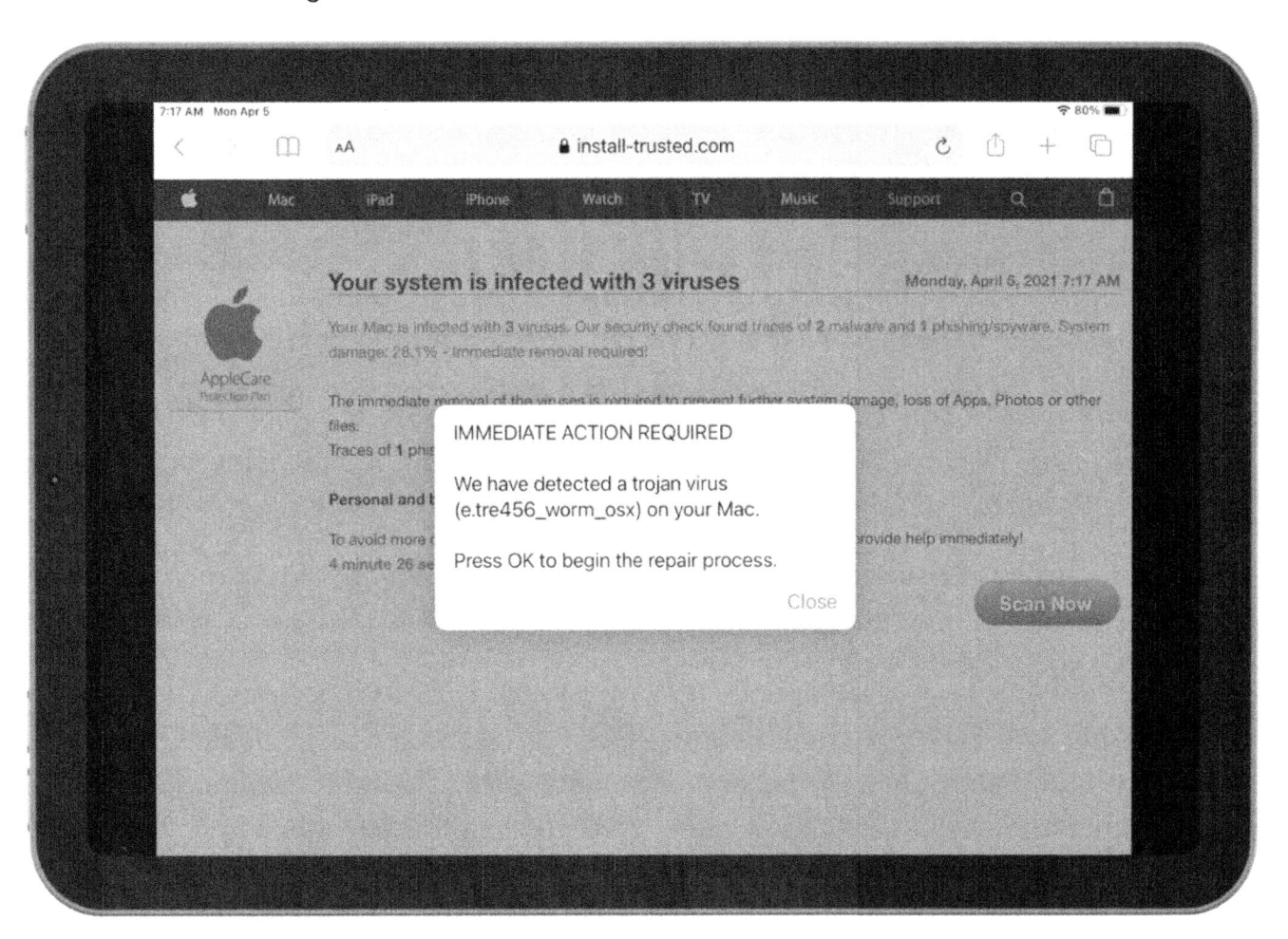

Spotting the Warning Signs

Scams often share telltale signs. Here's how to identify potential threats:

1. **Urgency or Fear:** Messages that pressure you to act immediately—like claiming your account will be suspended or your device compromised—are red flags.

2. **Requests for Personal Information**: Legitimate organizations rarely request sensitive information, such as passwords or credit card numbers, through email or text.

3. **Unfamiliar Senders**: Be cautious of emails or messages from unknown senders, particularly those that include links or attachments.

4. **Grammar and Spelling Errors**: Many scams originate from overseas and often contain errors in language or formatting.

5. **Too-Good-to-Be-True Offers**: If something sounds too good to be true—like a prize or unexpected inheritance—it likely is.

Protecting Yourself from Scams

Taking simple precautions can significantly reduce your risk of falling victim to scams:

1. **Verify Before You Trust**: If you receive an unexpected email or message, don't click links or open attachments right away. Instead, contact the organization directly using their official website or phone number to confirm authenticity.

2. **Use Strong Passwords**: Protect your online accounts with unique, strong passwords. Consider using Apple's built-in Keychain feature to generate and store secure passwords.

3. **Enable Two-Factor Authentication (2FA)**: For added security, enable 2FA on your Apple ID and other important accounts. This feature requires a second verification step, such as a code sent to your device, making it harder for scammers to access your accounts.

4. **Stay Up to Date**: Regularly update your iPad's software to ensure you have the latest security patches. To check for updates, go to Settings > General > Software Update.

5. **Install Apps from Trusted Sources**: Only download apps from the official App Store to avoid fake or malicious software.

6. **Avoid Sharing Personal Information**: Be cautious about sharing personal details online, even on social media. Scammers can use this information to target you.

What to Do If You Suspect a Scam

If you encounter something suspicious, follow these steps to protect yourself:

1. **Don't Engage**: Avoid responding to emails, messages, or calls that seem questionable.

2. **Report the Incident**:

    - For phishing emails, forward them to reportphishing@apple.com (if Apple-related) or the legitimate company's fraud department.

    - Report scams to https://reportfraud.ftc.gov/, the Federal Trade Commission's online fraud reporting site.

3. **Run a Security Check**: If you've clicked a suspicious link or shared information, change your passwords immediately and monitor your accounts for unusual activity. Consider running a security scan on your iPad with Apple's built-in tools or a trusted antivirus app.

4. **Block and Delete**: Use your iPad's Block Contact feature to prevent further messages from the sender. Delete the suspicious message or email afterward.

Practicing Safe Online Habits

Building good online habits can keep you safe in the long run:

- **Hover Over Links**: Before clicking a link, hold your finger over it (but don't click) to preview the destination URL. Ensure it matches the official website.

- **Secure Wi-Fi Use**: When using public Wi-Fi, avoid logging into accounts or entering sensitive information. If needed, use a VPN (Virtual Private Network) for secure browsing.

- **Be Skeptical**: Trust your instincts. If something feels off or too good to be true, take extra caution.

- **Educate Yourself**: Stay informed about the latest scams. Many organizations, like the Federal Trade Commission (FTC), regularly update resources to help you recognize and avoid new threats.

Scams can seem intimidating, but with knowledge and vigilance, you can stay one step ahead of fraudsters. By recognizing the warning signs and taking proactive measures, you'll significantly reduce your risk of falling victim to scams. Most importantly, remember that it's okay to take your time—legitimate organizations won't pressure you into immediate action.

Backing Up Your Data to iCloud and Staying Protected

Backing up your iPad ensures that your precious memories, important documents, and personalized settings are safe in case of unexpected events like losing your device, accidental deletion, or technical issues. Apple's **iCloud** provides a seamless, reliable, and secure way to back up your data automatically. In this sub-chapter, we'll guide you through setting up iCloud backups, managing storage efficiently, and using best practices to protect your data.

Why Backups Are Essential

Backing up your data is like creating a safety net for your digital life. Here's why it matters:

- **Device Loss or Damage**: If your iPad is lost, stolen, or damaged, you can recover your information on a new device.

- **Accidental Deletions**: Backups let you restore important photos, files, or settings if you delete them unintentionally.

- **Effortless Transition**: When upgrading to a new iPad, backups make transferring your data quick and easy.

Apple's iCloud is an excellent option because it integrates directly with your iPad, automating the backup process and keeping your data secure.

Setting Up iCloud Backup

Follow these steps to enable iCloud Backup and ensure your data is protected:

1. **Sign in to iCloud**
    - Open the **Settings** app.
    - Tap your name at the top of the screen (Apple ID).
    - Make sure you're signed in with your Apple ID. If not, sign in or create one.

2. **Turn On iCloud Backup**
    - In the **Apple ID** menu, select **iCloud**.
    - Scroll down and tap **iCloud Backup**.
    - Toggle the **iCloud Backup** switch to **On**.
    - Tap **Back Up Now** to manually create your first backup.

3. **Set Up Automatic Backups**
    - iCloud automatically backs up your iPad when it's connected to Wi-Fi, charging, and locked. This ensures your data is updated regularly without requiring manual intervention.

Managing iCloud Storage

iCloud provides 5 GB of free storage, but you might need more space depending on your needs. Here's how to manage your storage effectively:

1. **View Storage Usage**

   - Go to **Settings > [Your Name] > iCloud > Manage Account Storage**.
   - Review the space used by backups, photos, documents, and other apps.

2. **Upgrade Your iCloud Plan**

   - If you need more storage, tap **Change Storage Plan** in the **Manage Account Storage** menu.
   - Choose a plan that suits your needs:
     - **50 GB**: Ideal for personal backups.
     - **200 GB**: Suitable for families or those with extensive data.
     - **2 TB**: Perfect for heavy users or those managing multiple devices.

3. **Optimize Storage Usage**

   - Disable backups for apps you don't need in **Settings > iCloud > Manage Account Storage**.
   - Regularly clean up old backups from unused devices.

Best Practices for Keeping Your Data Safe

Your backups are only as secure as the precautions you take. Here are some tips to maximize protection:

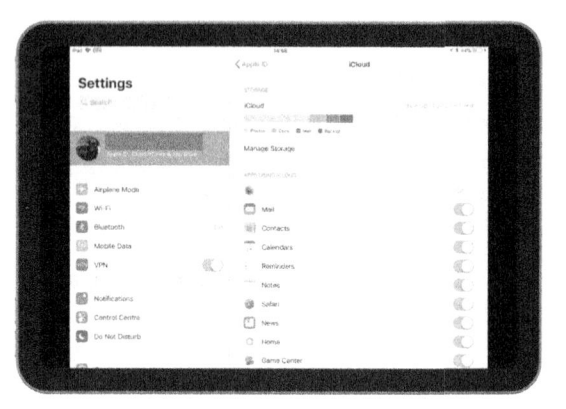

1. **Use a Strong Apple ID Password**
   - Ensure your Apple ID password is unique and hard to guess. Avoid common passwords or using personal information.

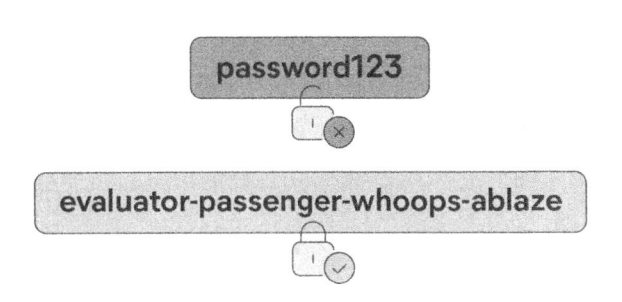

2. **Enable Two-Factor Authentication (2FA)**
   - Two-factor authentication enhances security by requiring a verification code along with your password. To enable it:
     - Go to **Settings** > **[Your Name]** > **Password & Security** > **Turn On Two-Factor Authentication**.

3. **Secure Your iPad**
   - Use **Face ID** or **Touch ID** for quick yet secure access to your device.
   - Set a strong passcode by going to **Settings > Face ID & Passcode** (or Touch ID & Passcode).

4. **Beware of Phishing Attempts**
   - Be cautious of emails or messages claiming to be from Apple, especially those requesting your password or personal details. Always verify directly through **Settings > Apple ID** or **Apple's official website**.

5. **Regularly Check Your Backups**
   - Occasionally, confirm that your iPad is backing up properly. Go to **Settings > [Your Name] > iCloud > iCloud Backup** to verify the last backup date.

Restoring from an iCloud Backup

If you ever need to restore your iPad or set up a new one, follow these steps:

1. **During Initial Setup**:
   - When prompted, choose Restore from iCloud Backup.
   - Sign in with your Apple ID and select the most recent backup.

2. **After Setup**:
   - To restore after setup, you'll need to erase the device first. **Go to Settings > General > Transfer or Reset iPad > Erase All Content and Settings**, then choose **Restore from iCloud Backup** during the setup process.

Restoring from an iCloud backup is straightforward and ensures you're back up and running in no time.

Backing up your iPad to iCloud provides peace of mind and ensures that your important data is safe, accessible, and easily recoverable. By setting up automatic backups, managing your storage efficiently, and following security best practices, you can confidently use your iPad without worrying about losing valuable information.

Advanced Tips and Tricks

Customizing Your iPad with Settings and Widgets

One of the most enjoyable aspects of using an iPad is making it truly your own. Customizing settings and adding widgets allows you to tailor your device to your needs, preferences, and daily routine. In this sub-chapter, you'll learn how to adjust key settings, organize your Home Screen, and leverage widgets to access important information at a glance—all while enhancing functionality and creating a personalized experience.

Exploring the Settings App

The **Settings app** is the command center for customizing your iPad. Here's how to navigate it effectively:

1. **Opening the Settings App**

    - Tap the gray **Settings** icon on your **Home Screen**. The left-hand menu provides categories, while the right-hand pane shows options for the selected category.

2. **Key Settings to Customize**

    - **Wallpaper**: Change your iPad's background to a favorite photo or Apple's dynamic options. Go to **Settings > Wallpaper > Choose a New Wallpaper**. Select an image and tap **Set for Home Screen, Lock Screen, or both**.

    - **Display Brightness**: Adjust screen brightness and enable **True Tone** or **Night Shift** for comfortable viewing. Go to **Settings > Display & Brightness**.

    - **Sounds**: Customize alert tones for calls, emails, and messages in **Settings > Sounds & Haptics**.

    - **Privacy**: Control app permissions (like camera or location access) in **Settings > Privacy & Security**.

3. **Arranging App Preferences**
   Scroll down in the Settings menu to find app-specific options. Here, you can tweak how individual apps behave, such as notifications, data usage, or syncing.

Organizing Your Home Screen

Your Home Screen is the gateway to everything on your iPad. Keeping it tidy and functional is key to navigating your device efficiently.

1. **Rearranging Apps**

    - Tap and hold any app icon until the icons jiggle.

    - Drag the app to a new location or another page.

    - To create a folder, drag one app onto another. Name the folder when prompted and add more apps by dragging them into it.

2. **Removing Apps from the Home Screen**

    - Tap and hold an app until the menu appears.

    - Select **Remove App** and choose **Remove** from **Home Screen** to keep the app but declutter the display.

3. **Using the App Library**

    - Swipe left past your last **Home Screen** to access the **App Library**, which organizes all your apps automatically. You can search or browse categories here.

Customizing with Widgets

Widgets provide at-a-glance information directly on your Home Screen or Today View (accessed by swiping right from the Home Screen). Here's how to make the most of them:

1. **Adding Widgets**

    - Tap and hold an empty space on the Home Screen until the apps jiggle.

- Tap the + icon in the upper-left corner.

- Browse available widgets by scrolling or searching.

- Tap a widget to preview its size options, then tap **Add Widget** to place it on your screen.

2. **Editing Widgets**

    - Tap and hold a widget to open the editing menu.

    - Select **Edit Widget** to adjust its settings (e.g., changing the city for a Weather widget).

    - Drag widgets to rearrange them or group them into a **Stack** by dragging one on top of another. Stacks allow you to swipe between multiple widgets in the same space.

3. **Essential Widgets for Seniors**

    - **Weather**: Stay updated on current conditions and forecasts.

    - **Calendar**: Quickly view upcoming appointments.

    - **Battery**: Monitor your iPad and connected device battery levels.

    - **News**: Catch up on the latest headlines at a glance.

Using Focus Modes for Personalization

Focus modes let you tailor notifications and Home Screen layouts based on your activity or time of day:

1. **Setting Up a Focus Mode**

    - Go to **Settings > Focus** and tap **+** to create a new mode (e.g., Work or Relaxation).

    - Choose which people and apps can notify you during this mode.

2. **Customizing Home Screens for Focus Modes**
    - Assign specific Home Screen pages to appear when a Focus mode is active. For example, distracting apps can be hidden during work mode, and entertainment apps can be shown during relaxation mode.

Accessibility Settings for Ease of Use

Apple includes powerful accessibility options to make your iPad easier to use:

1. **Larger Text and Icons**
    - Adjust the text size in **Settings > Display & Brightness > Text Size**. Use **Bold Text** for better visibility.
    - Enable **Zoom** in **Settings > Accessibility** to magnify parts of the screen.

2. **Voice Control and Assistive Touch**
    - Use **Voice Control** to navigate hands-free. Enable it in **Settings > Accessibility > Voice Control**.
    - Enable **AssistiveTouch** to add an on-screen button for common tasks like returning to the Home Screen.

3. **Hearing and Vision Assistance**
    - Adjust sound balance or enable subtitles in **Settings > Accessibility > Hearing Devices**.
    - Turn on **VoiceOver** for spoken descriptions of screen elements.

Customizing your iPad is about making it work for you. Whether it's organizing apps, adding widgets, or exploring accessibility features, taking the time to personalize your device enhances both its functionality and your experience.

Multitasking and Using Split Screen for Productivity

The iPad is a powerful tool for staying productive, and its multitasking capabilities make managing multiple tasks easier than ever. With features like Split View, Slide Over, and Picture-in-Picture, you can use your iPad like a pro to get more done in less time. In this sub-chapter, we'll walk you through each of these multitasking tools, providing step-by-step instructions to help you harness their full potential.

Understanding iPad Multitasking Basics

Multitasking on the iPad allows you to use multiple apps simultaneously, making it ideal for tasks like comparing documents, taking notes during a video call, or referencing a web page while writing an email.

Key Multitasking Features

1. **Split View**: Display two apps side by side.
2. **Slide Over**: Open a smaller, floating app window over your current app.
3. **Picture-in-Picture (PiP)**: Continue watching a video or participating in a FaceTime call while using other apps.

Using Split View

Split View lets you work in two apps at the same time, dividing your screen into two adjustable sections. Here's how to set it up:

1. **Open Split View**
    - Start by opening an app, such as Safari.
    - Swipe up from the bottom of the screen to reveal the Dock.
    - Drag a second app icon from the **Dock** to the right or left edge of the screen until it "snaps" into place.

2. **Adjust Split View Sizes**

    - Drag the divider between the two apps to resize each section. You can choose a 50-50 split or allocate more space to one app.

3. **Switch Apps in Split View**

    - Swipe down on the top of either app in **Split View** to replace it with another app.

4. **Close Split View**

    - Drag the divider all the way to one side to return to a single app view.

Using Slide Over

Slide Over is perfect for quickly checking an app without leaving your current task. It opens a smaller, floating window that you can move or hide.

1. **Open Slide Over**

    - Open an app and swipe up to reveal the **Dock.**
    - Drag a second app onto the center of the screen, and it will appear in a smaller window.

2. **Move and Hide the Slide Over Window**

    - Drag the **Slide Over** window to either side of the screen.
    - Swipe it off the edge of the screen to hide it temporarily. Swipe from the edge again to bring it back.

3. **Switch Apps in Slide Over**

    - Swipe left or right at the bottom of the **Slide Over** window to switch between apps.

Using Picture-in-Picture

Picture-in-Picture (PiP) is great for watching videos or participating in FaceTime calls while using other apps.

1. **Enable PiP**
   - Start a video in an app like Safari or FaceTime.
   - Tap the **Picture-in-Picture icon** (a small rectangle with an arrow) to shrink the video into a movable window.

2. **Move and Resize the PiP Window**
   - Drag the window to any corner of the screen.
   - Pinch with two fingers to resize it.

3. **Minimize or Close PiP**
   - Drag the PiP window to the edge of the screen to minimize it.
   - Tap the **X** to close it entirely.

Combining Multitasking Features

The iPad's multitasking tools can be used together for maximum efficiency. For instance:

- Use **Split View** to work in two apps while a third app is in **Slide Over**.
- Watch a video in **Picture-in-Picture** while you work in **Split View**.

Example Scenario

Imagine you're researching a topic. You can:

1. Open Safari in Split View with the Notes app to jot down ideas.
2. Add Slide Over to check emails without disrupting your workflow.
3. Use Picture-in-Picture to watch a tutorial video related to your research.

Customizing Multitasking Settings

Fine-tune your multitasking experience in the **Settings** app:

1. Go to **Settings > Home Screen & Multitasking > Multitasking**.

2. Toggle features like **Allow Multiple Apps** and **Picture-in-Picture** on or off based on your preferences.

Tips for Seniors to Master Multitasking

- **Practice with Simple Tasks**: Start with tasks like opening Safari and Notes in Split View to get comfortable with multitasking gestures.

- **Use the Dock Strategically**: Keep frequently used apps in the **Dock** for quick access.

- **Be Patient**: Multitasking gestures may feel tricky at first, but regular practice will make them second nature.

Multitasking transforms your iPad into a productivity powerhouse. Whether you're managing emails, planning an event, or enjoying your favorite shows, mastering these tools will help you make the most of your time.

Troubleshooting Common Issues and Finding Help

No matter how well you use your iPad, occasional hiccups may arise. Fortunately, Apple has designed the iPad to be user-friendly when resolving issues. This sub-chapter will guide you through addressing common problems, applying basic troubleshooting techniques, and finding the right help when needed.

Understanding Common iPad Issues

Here are some frequent problems iPad users encounter:

1. **Unresponsive Apps or Screen**: Apps might freeze or crash, or the screen may not respond to touch.

2. **Wi-Fi Connectivity Issues**: Difficulty connecting to Wi-Fi networks or maintaining a stable connection.

3. **Battery Draining Quickly**: The device not holding a charge as expected.

4. **Storage Problems**: Running out of space to download apps or save files.

By understanding the root cause, you can approach troubleshooting more effectively.

Common iPad Issues and How to Resolve Them

Here are a few common challenges iPad users might encounter, along with simple solutions:

Unresponsive Apps or Screen

When an app freezes or the screen stops responding:

- **Force Quit the App**:
    - Open the App Switcher by swiping up from the bottom of the screen or double-pressing the Home button on older models.
    - Locate the problematic app and swipe it upward to close it.
- **Restart the iPad**:
    - **For iPads with a Home button**: Hold the Top button until the "Slide to Power Off" option appears. Drag the slider and restart.
    - **For iPads without a Home button**: Press and hold the Top button and either Volume button until the slider appears.

Wi-Fi Connectivity Problems

If your iPad isn't connecting to Wi-Fi:

- **Check your Wi-Fi Settings**:
    1. Go to **Settings > Wi-Fi**.
    2. Ensure the correct network is selected and the password is entered correctly.
- **Reset Network Settings**:
    1. Navigate to **Settings > General > Transfer** or **Reset iPad > Reset > Reset Network Settings**.

2. Reconnect to your Wi-Fi network.

Battery Draining Too Quickly

A rapidly depleting battery can be frustrating:

- **Adjust your settings**:

    1. Lower the screen brightness under **Settings > Display & Brightness**.

    2. Turn on **Low Power Mode** via **Settings > Battery**.

- **Check for battery-draining apps**:

    1. Visit **Settings > Battery** to view app usage.

iPad Not Responding to Updates

If your iPad isn't installing updates:

- Ensure you have enough storage by visiting **Settings > General > iPad Storage**.

- Connect to a stable Wi-Fi network and try updating again through **Settings > General > Software Update**.

Advanced Troubleshooting Tools

If the basics don't resolve the issue, consider these advanced methods:

Reset All Settings

- Navigate to **Settings > General > Transfer or Reset iPad > Reset > Reset All Settings**. This won't delete your data but will reset configurations like Wi-Fi passwords.

Restore Your iPad Using iTunes or Finder

- Connect your iPad to a computer and use iTunes (Windows) or Finder (Mac) to restore it to factory settings. Always back up your data first.

Check for Hardware Issues

- If your iPad is overheating, won't charge, or has visible damage, contact Apple Support or visit an authorized repair center.

Finding Help When Needed

If troubleshooting steps don't solve the problem, there are plenty of resources available:

Apple Support App

The Apple Support app is pre-installed on your iPad and provides tailored troubleshooting advice, helpful articles, and the ability to schedule a repair or chat with a specialist.

Visit the Apple Support Website

Head to ***support.apple.com*** for detailed articles, FAQs, and instructional videos covering nearly every iPad issue.

Contact Apple Directly

- Use the Apple Support app to initiate a phone call or live chat with an expert.
- Schedule an appointment at your nearest Apple Store or Authorized Service Provider for in-person assistance.

Community Forums

Apple's Community Discussions is an excellent place to seek advice from other users who may have experienced and solved similar issues.

Proactive Tips to Minimize Future Problems

1. **Keep Your Software Updated**:
   Enable automatic updates via **Settings > General > Software Update > Automatic Updates** to stay ahead of potential bugs.

2. **Back Up Your Data Regularly**:
   Use iCloud or your computer to back up your iPad, ensuring that your information is safe even if the device encounters issues.

3. **Monitor Your Storage**:
   Keep tabs on your storage under **Settings > General > iPad Storage**, deleting unused apps or files to prevent performance slowdowns.

Confidence Through Preparedness

Troubleshooting doesn't need to be daunting. By following these steps and knowing where to find help, you'll feel empowered to resolve issues swiftly and effectively. With just a bit of practice, you'll master your iPad's quirks and enjoy a smoother, stress-free experience every day.

FAQs

Here are some frequently asked questions about troubleshooting your iPad, grouped by common issues, along with solutions to help you resolve them:

Performance Issues

My iPad is running slowly. How can I speed it up?

- **Solution:**
  - **Free up storage**: Check if you're running low on storage by going to **Settings > General > iPad Storage**. Delete unused apps or large files like photos, videos, or documents.
  - **Close unused apps**: Swipe up from the bottom of the screen to open the **App Switcher** and swipe away apps you're not using.
  - **Clear Safari cache**: Go to **Settings > Safari > Clear History and Website Data**.
  - **Restart your iPad**: Turn it off and back on to refresh the system.

Why is my iPad's battery draining too quickly?

- **Solution:**
  - **Check battery usage**: Go to **Settings > Battery** to see which apps are using the most battery. Consider disabling notifications or background refresh for these apps.
  - **Adjust brightness**: Reduce screen brightness or enable **Auto-Brightness** in **Settings > Accessibility > Display & Text Size**.
  - **Enable Low Power Mode**: Go to **Settings > Battery** and toggle on **Low Power Mode** to extend battery life.

Connectivity Issues

I can't connect to Wi-Fi. What should I do?

- **Solution:**

    - **Check Wi-Fi settings**: Go to **Settings > Wi-Fi** and ensure you are connected to the correct network.

    - **Restart your router**: Sometimes, resetting your router can fix connectivity issues.

    - **Forget and reconnect to the network**: In **Settings > Wi-Fi**, tap the "i" next to your network, then select **Forget This Network** and reconnect.

    - **Reset network settings**: Go to **Settings > General > Reset > Reset Network Settings**.

My Bluetooth is not working. How can I fix it?

- **Solution:**

    - **Toggle Bluetooth off and on**: Go to **Settings > Bluetooth** and turn it off and back on.

    - **Forget and reconnect devices**: In the Bluetooth settings, tap the "i" next to the device and select **Forget This Device**, then reconnect.

    - **Reset network settings**: If Bluetooth still doesn't work, go to **Settings > General > Reset > Reset Network Settings**.

App Issues

My apps are crashing or not opening. What can I do?

- **Solution:**

    - **Update your apps**: Go to the App Store, tap your profile icon, and check for updates.

- o **Restart your iPad**: A simple restart can resolve many app-related issues.

- o **Reinstall the app**: If the problem persists, uninstall the app and reinstall it from the App Store.

- o **Clear app cache (if supported)**: Some apps allow clearing cached data from within the app settings.

An app I want to use isn't downloading. What can I try?

- Solution:

    - o **Check Wi-Fi and storage**: Ensure you're connected to Wi-Fi and have enough storage space.

    - o **Sign in to your Apple ID**: Go to **Settings > [Your Name] > iTunes & App Store** and ensure you're signed in with the correct Apple ID.

    - o **Restart the App Store**: Close the App Store and reopen it. If this doesn't work, restart your iPad.

    - o **Check the App Store status**: Sometimes, the App Store may be down. Visit Apple's System Status page to check.

Display and Touchscreen Issues

My iPad screen is unresponsive. How do I fix it?

- Solution:

    - o **Clean the screen**: Dirt and moisture can make the touchscreen unresponsive. Clean it gently with a soft, lint-free cloth.

    - o **Force restart**: Press and release the **Volume Up** button, press and release the **Volume Down** button, then press and hold the **Power** button until the Apple logo appears.

    - o **Check for screen protectors:** If you're using a screen protector, ensure it's not interfering with the touchscreen.

- **Reset settings**: If the problem persists, go to **Settings > General > Reset > Reset All Settings** (this won't erase your data, but will reset personalized settings).

iCloud and Backup Issues

My iCloud backup isn't working. What can I do?

- **Solution:**

    - **Check iCloud settings**: Go to **Settings > [Your Name] > iCloud** and ensure iCloud Backup is enabled.

    - **Check your Wi-Fi connection**: Backups require a stable Wi-Fi connection. Ensure you're connected to Wi-Fi.

    - **Free up iCloud storage**: Go to **Settings > [Your Name] > iCloud > Manage Storage** to see if you have enough space for the backup.

    - **Manual backup**: If automatic backup is failing, you can manually initiate a backup by going to **Settings > [Your Name] > iCloud > iCloud Backup**, then tap **Back Up Now**.

How do I restore my iPad from an iCloud backup?

- **Solution:**

    - **Erase your iPad**: Go to **Settings > General > Reset > Erase All Content and Settings**.

    - **Restore during setup**: When you set up your iPad again, select **Restore from iCloud Backup** and choose the backup you want to restore from.

Miscellaneous Issues

My iPad is stuck on the Apple logo. How do I fix it?

- **Solution**:

    - **Force restart**: As mentioned above, force restart your iPad by pressing and releasing the **Volume Up** button, pressing and releasing the **Volume Down** button, and then holding the **Power** button until the Apple logo appears.

    - **Restore through iTunes**: If the issue persists, connect your iPad to a computer with iTunes installed. Select your device in iTunes and click **Restore iPad**.

How do I find help if none of these solutions work?

- **Solution:**

    - **Contact Apple Support**: You can reach out to Apple Support via the **Apple Support app** or by visiting the **Apple Support website**.

    - **Visit an Apple Store**: If possible, schedule an appointment at your nearest Apple Store for a hands-on diagnostic.

    - **Use Apple's online resources**: Visit the **Apple Support website** for step-by-step guides and troubleshooting articles.

With these solutions, you should be able to resolve common iPad issues on your own. If problems persist, Apple's customer support team is always available to assist you further.

Conclusion

Congratulations on completing this iPad user guide! By now, you've learned the ins and outs of setting up, navigating, and personalizing your iPad. You've explored its powerful apps, mastered multitasking, discovered tips for productivity, and gained insights into using your device securely and efficiently. Whether you're using your iPad for work, creativity, communication, or leisure, you now have the tools to make the most of this versatile device.

Remember, your iPad is a dynamic tool that continues to evolve with software updates and new features. Don't hesitate to explore, experiment, and learn more as you go. With its vast capabilities and ease of use, your iPad can adapt to your unique needs and help you stay connected, productive, and entertained.

For further assistance, revisit sections of this guide, check the FAQ for quick solutions, or consult Apple Support for more complex issues. With this guide as your companion, you're fully equipped to enjoy the endless possibilities your iPad offers.

Thank you for choosing this guide, and happy exploring!

Steve Carren

Bonus

Grab your FREE copy of "iPad Essentials" and complete common Tasks like Shopping, Banking, Creativity, and Art.

Make the most of your iPad Experience!

https://sunshine-forest.org/ipad-seniors-guide-bonus/

Printed in Dunstable, United Kingdom